Global Culture and its Future

Dago Steenis

Global Culture and its Future

Letters to set you thinking

Global Culture and its Future

Amersfoortsestraat 27, 3769 AD Soesterberg, The Netherlands
info@uitgeverijaspekt.nl – http://www.uitgeverijaspekt.nl

Cover Design: Jaap Kooy, Den Haag
Foto author: Foto-atelier Ab Hofstra, Pingjum
Inside: Uitgeverij Aspekt

ISBN: 9789461534002
NUR: 736

Printed and bound by CPI Group (UK) Ltd, Croydon, CR0 4YY

To Ria

By way of introduction

I have written these letters because I am concerned. What am I concerned about? I am concerned about the state of the world. I care about the future: not the future of a particular nation or continent, or the future of a particular people or religion, but the future of humankind.

The future looks increasingly unsure. I see increasing disparity between rich and poor, increasing environmental pollution, increasing energy shortage, increasing threat of pandemics, increasing destruction of nature, increasing pressure on food and water security, and all of this happening against a backdrop of climate change. These problems can only be overcome by a united humanity.

Is humanity united? When I look around me I see a global community that is divided to the core. Divided into groups, nations, military alliances, religions, classes, ideologies, traditions, you name it. I see a global community increasingly disintegrating into factional conflict. Every day we hear about corruption, dishonest gain, the drug trade, crime, oppression, war, terrorism, looting, human trafficking, violence and rape. Far too many people are caught up in a relentless pursuit of wealth and power and seek to oppress those who stand in their way.

This unbridled pursuit of desire that will stop at nothing bears testament to man's animal origins, which is hardly surprising given that man spent hundreds of thousands of years living as an animal among animals. Historians may tell us that we have been 'civilized' for thousands years. But that all depends on what they mean by 'civilization'.

My personal experiences of what historians refer to as civilization have not been that positive. During the German occupation of the Netherlands the occupying forces deported my maternal relatives and had them put to death in an appalling manner. Some six million men, women and children suffered a similar fate at the hands of their supposedly civilized contemporaries. This occurred during a war in which, over a period of five years, people of my generation caused some 70 million of their fellow human beings to die a miserable death. So, again, I say that all depends on what they mean by 'civilization'.

What I am calling for is for us to become acutely aware of one thing. There are still too many among us who have no trouble making horrifying plans. And too many others allow themselves to be used as instruments by those intent on committing monstrous acts. Some carry out terrorist attacks, others allow themselves to be trained as soldiers and go on to become professional killers who perform their bloody work without mercy, without a second thought, and sometimes even with pleasure.

It is time for us to stop turning a blind eye to reality. People are often still guided by their baser animal tendencies: they still act and think in primitive ways. We cannot begin to build a better, less primitive, society until we acknowledge that this is the case. Statesmen of the more than two hundred countries on the world map continue to threaten each other with military action. They follow the example set by leaders of the superpowers, the warlords on the current world stage, who believe themselves to be invincible because they possess nuclear weapons.

Our era is characterised by a widespread sense of unease which manifests in the form of protests. The riots, uprisings, strikes and demonstrations are not simply voicing dissent fuelled by a financial and economic crisis. All over the world we are seeing opposition to authority. The masses are no longer as submissive as they once were. The call for change is getting louder.

All of this is leading to growing violence on all sides. Wouldn't it be preferable for us to develop our better qualities as human beings, our truly human qualities? I have reflected on the road we need to travel to create a more truly humane society that is united and at peace.

Dago Steenis, The Hague, April 2013

Starting points

1

Viewing humankind and culture from a distance

Dear Contemporaries,

I have spent much of my intellectual life trying to find a new way of thinking, a new worldview, a new vision of humankind and a new vision of society.

I have always adhered to the principle that, in this endeavour, it is necessary to view things from a certain remove or distance. The people involved in a revolution see only chaos. But historians who look back on the events many years later have sufficient overview to comprehend what happened: their vantage point of greater distance enables them to separate the essential factors from incidental circumstances in order to gain insight. Only then is it possible to offer a structural explanation of what happened. In other words, only overview affords insight, and it is only possible to gain an overview with the perspective afforded by distance.

This is actually quite logical. If you are lying in long grass, you see nothing but stalks. If you sit up, you see a field. If you stand up, you see that the field is in a valley surrounded by mountains. If you climb a mountain you see a mountain landscape. From an aircraft you see that the mountains form part of a range of mountains. Yet from a spaceship you realise that what you have been looking at is actually a spherical celestial body, a planet. You lose sight of the details: rather than being preoccupied with a particular region or country, you see the earth as a whole as the home of humanity. The astronaut has a perspective that other people lack: the earth is a beautiful planet. From the perspective of outer space, the battles fought out by the people far below are seen as insignificant affairs.

In other words, the greater the distance, the broader the overview, and the broader the overview, the deeper the insight. Or, to state it more concisely, distance is a prerequisite for insight and understanding. This is a universally valid principle. It holds true for the cosmologist and the biologist, and it holds equally true for those who want to gain insight into and understand human society and culture.

I treat this as a golden rule. To view the past from a distance it is necessary to focus on long-term patterns. How does this apply when examining the phenomenon of culture? Well, as far as I am concerned, it requires that we examine culture over the longest possible period, as a process of evolution from its origins to the present day.

As you can see, I am not talking about human history: my area of interest is the cultural evolution of humanity. I am essentially calling for the recognition of a new discipline of 'science of culture'.

Why this new term? How will this new discipline add to our understanding? To explain this, I would like to recount something that happened back in 1945, when I enrolled at the University of Amsterdam to study history. Among the faculty that taught me was Jan Romein, a history professor who initiated a new approach to the study of history in the form of theoretical history. He believed that history developed according to its own laws.

In my view, in adopting this approach, Romein began moving in a direction that led him away from the tradition that writes history as narrative. His fellow faculty members did not follow suit. I think they were right not to do so. For although Romein continued to call himself a historian, he had actually inadvertently initiated an entirely new discipline, which I call 'science of culture': a discipline that studies human culture as an evolutionary process that unfolds according to the laws that govern all evolutionary processes.

So, what might the study of cultural evolution involve?

2

The evolution of culture: from animal to human

Dear Contemporaries,

Romein's approach to human history meant that he studied culture as a general phenomenon of human existence. He looked at what cultures (or civilizations as they are referred to by historians) have in common, rather than the ways in which they differ.

This can be compared with the scientific approach to the phenomenon of life. Zoologists who study the animal kingdom and botanists who study the plant kingdom concentrate on individual forms of life. But it is also possible to study the phenomenon of life itself, which is what biologists do. Rather than focusing on the ways in which the countless forms through which life manifests differ, they look at what all forms of life have in common.

To be able to do this it is necessary to view things from a sufficient distance. Then it becomes clear that the phenomenon of life has undergone a long process of development: there has been a process of evolution. Then you can trace the origins of life to find out the direction in which biotic evolution is heading.

To pursue the metaphor, while historians study individual cultures, cultural scientists would seek to identify what the many forms in which culture manifests have in common. To be able to do this again it is necessary to view things from a sufficient distance. Then it becomes clear that human culture has undergone a long process of development: there has been a process of evolution. Then you can examine how culture originated and the direction in which culture is evolving.

I myself have embarked on this task and there are several things that I have discovered.

There were human species that became extinct. At this point the only surviving human species is Homo sapiens, to which all current human beings belong. All human species, including Homo sapiens, are animal species – they originally lived as animals among animals. I call the period prior to the point at which human existence began to differentiate from a purely animal existence the Animalium.

When we look at the evolution of the inner world of human nature, human thoughts and feelings, it is clear that the human species is becoming less animal and more human. This evolutionary process can be referred to as a process of humanisation. It is a development that is progressing steadily, albeit with a certain amount of trial and error along the way.

The only possible conclusion is that human beings are gradually evolving beyond their animal nature. When they are no longer ruled by their animal tendencies we will see the dawning of a new era in human existence that I call the Humanium.

But we still have some way to go before we reach that point. We current human beings exhibit both human and animal traits. We live in an era that is transitioning from the Animalium to the Humanium. I call this transitional era the Transitium.

The study of evolution as a general phenomenon makes it clear that development always occurs in stages. The transition from one stage to the next is often marked by a relatively brief period of crisis. The crisis is created by the battle between the old order, which does not want to give way, and the new order, which is forging ahead.

In terms of cultural evolution, the Transitium as a whole is a time of such crisis.

This is the era in which we live.

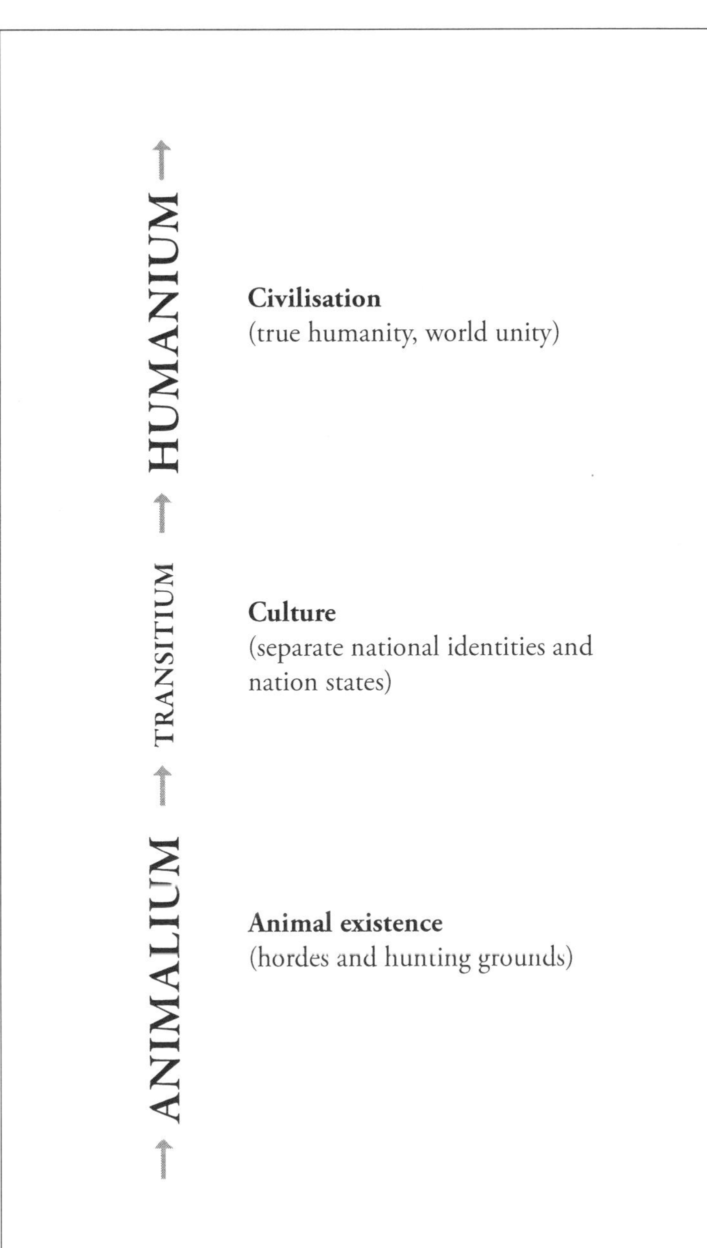
ANIMALIUM
TRANSITIUM
HUMANIUM
Civilisation
(true humanity, world unity)
Culture
(separate national identities and nation states)
Animal existence
(hordes and hunting grounds)

3

Humankind – the creator of culture

Dear Contemporaries,

Closer examination of the Animalium tells us that for approximately two to three million years human beings and their hominid ancestors were part of the animal kingdom. Yes, the animal kingdom. For even the most recent human species, Homo sapiens, did not differ from other animals when it came to securing food: like animals they hunted other animals and foraged for edible vegetation.

But human mammals were remarkable animals from the start. As a species they gradually developed a weapon that eventually allowed them to transcend the animal kingdom. That weapon was ingenuity.

Other animals also had weapons: natural weapons, such as claws, or tusks, or poisonous fangs, or the ability to leap or move at speed, or muscular strength, or camouflage, or the ability to hunt as a pack, or tremendous body weight, or wings. But, through their ingenuity, humans discovered how to equip themselves with self-devised and self-built weapons and tools.

These self-devised and self-built weapons and tools are known as artefacts. They served as artificial extensions of human muscle strength and dexterity. As well as using sticks and stones as weapons, early humans also made celts, catapults, spears, bows and arrows, built pit traps, mastered the use of fire and used animal hides to keep themselves warm. But even without these artefacts they used their ingenuity. To give an example: a group of humans making an alarming noise would drive a herd of horses in a certain direction. The frightened horses would gallop off, not realising that they were being driven towards the edge of a precipice. The whole herd would plummet off the edge of the precipice and sustain fatal injuries that made them easy prey. Human ingenuity made humans a superior animal. It was man, and not the lion, who became the king of the jungle.

But it didn't end there. The Transitium began to occur. There was a revolution in the evolution of the animal kingdom. Human beings were the revolutionaries. They discovered that they could ensure a more reliable food supply by producing it themselves. They started growing crops and keeping livestock and settled in villages and towns.

For hundreds of thousands of years human beings sought to make themselves more powerful. Then, approximately ten thousand years ago, they reached a decisive point in their development. The invention of agriculture and livestock farming enabled humans to definitively transcend the animal kingdom. As arable and livestock farmers they created a means of existence that was fundamentally different from animal existence. Humans created something that had not previously existed on earth: they created culture.

The creation of culture is probably the most radical revolution throughout the whole of human existence. The Transitium brought with it, from the beginning, the emergence of an essential difference between humans and animals.

Compared with other evolutionary phenomena the new phenomenon of culture developed very rapidly, especially the technical and material aspects of culture. Inventions, such as early writing systems, meant that human culture grew increasingly sophisticated. The inner world of human nature also became more complex as humans started questioning the mystery of life and death.

During the Transitium humans develop the characteristics that are typical of the human species.

Humans are becoming more human.

4

HOW MUCH LONGER WILL THE TRANSITIUM LAST?

Dear Contemporaries,

Cultural scientists are primarily concerned with the following questions: how far has humankind progressed along the road from animal existence to human existence? And when will humans have completely outgrown their animal nature?

To answer this question it is necessary to realise that the Transitium that is now occurring has actually lasted for a relatively brief period compared with the past and possible future of humankind. The human species that existed prior to Homo sapiens roamed the planet for two to three million years. Homo sapiens might still have many millions of years ahead of it.

In evolutionary terms, the ten thousand years that the Transitium has lasted to date is a relatively short period. This means that human culture still has to undergo considerable change before it becomes truly human. However, the fact that cultural evolution is progressing more rapidly than the natural evolutionary processes that preceded it gives cause for hope. And human culture also appears to be a self-accelerating process.

Having said that, it is also fair to say that humans themselves can influence how long the Transitium lasts. It is not by chance that humans became masters of the earth. They are more empowered than any other creature. They can interpret the world around them and they can also account for their own actions. They have large brains and great intellectual ability. In principle, they are in a position to determine the fate of the earth and the fate of the human species. So there is cause for optimism.

Yes, indeed. Ten thousand years of culture have made humans masters of the planet. The entire face of the earth is testament to human knowledge and knowhow. We can now build skyscrapers more than 500 metres high. We can also strip the earth of its mineral resources, exterminate species and empty the oceans of fish. We even have the capacity to obliterate ourselves from the surface of the planet with nuclear weapons.

As humans we are capable of achieving incredible things. But, given the current circumstances, are we sufficiently aware of our responsibility to nature and our fellow human beings?

As I have said, I am concerned. I see culture regressing. There is an urgent need for humankind to change its ways.

How can humankind do that? Well, first, the humanisation process needs to accelerate so the Transitium comes to an end, for, by definition, the Transitium will always be marred by motives and brutal acts that stem from our animal origins.

In the letters that follow I describe the primitive qualities that make human society an inhuman society.

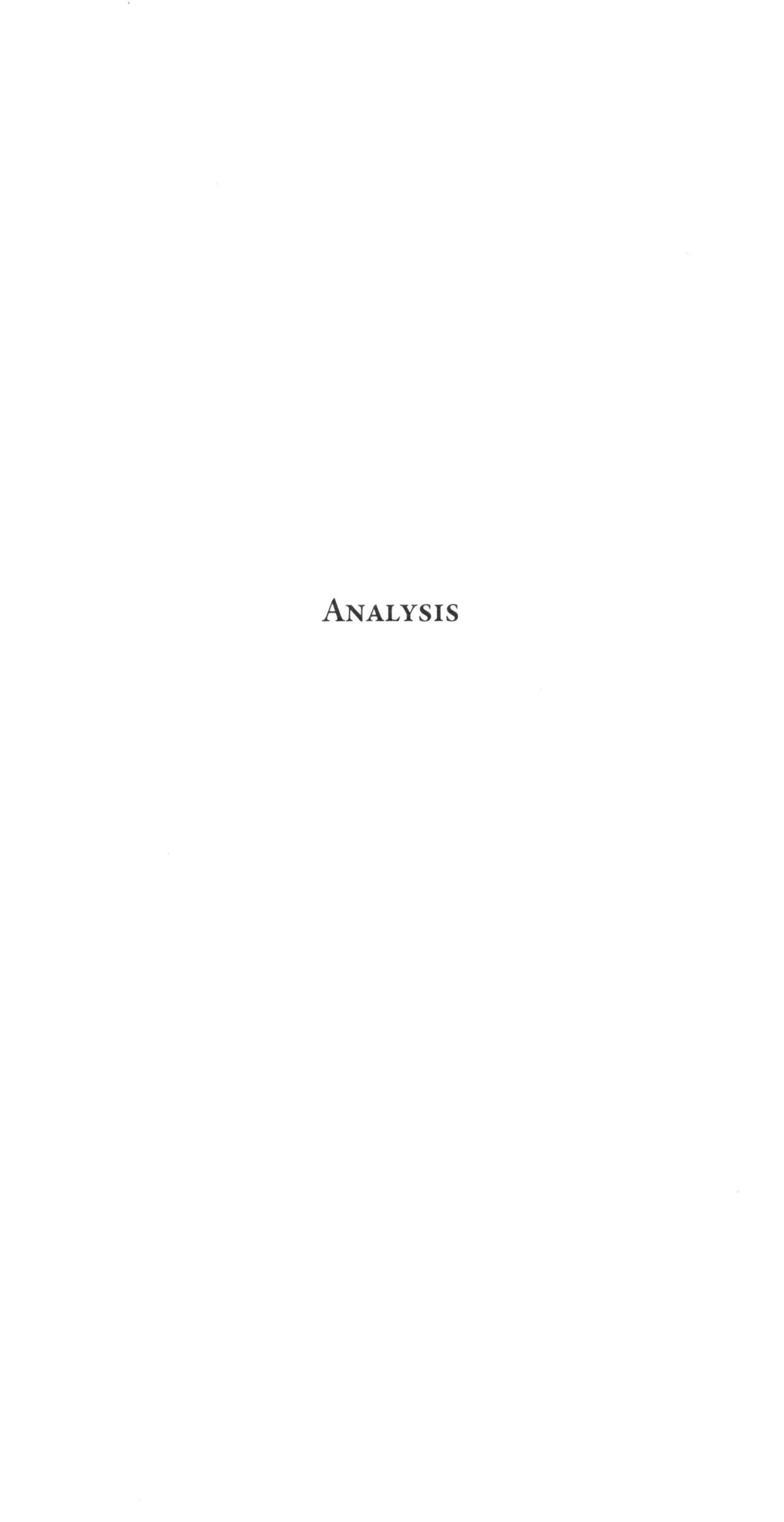

Analysis

5

A SHORT-LIVED CULTURE – AN INHUMAN SOCIETY!

Dear Contemporaries.

I suspect that few people realise how recently we emerged from the Animalium. Homo sapiens appeared on earth approximately two hundred thousand years ago. And, as we have seen, the earliest forms of agriculture and livestock farming (in other words, the earliest forms of culture) arose approximately ten thousand years ago.

The best way to gain a sense of the relatively recent emergence of culture is to visualise it as a point on a timeline. If we say that ten centimetres represents a period of a hundred thousand years, the existence of Homo sapiens would be 20 centimetres long. The period from the origins of culture to the present day would be the last centimetre. The most ancient civilizations (Egypt, and Mesopotamia) developed 5,000 years ago (the last five millimetres). People realised that the earth is round five centuries ago (0.5 millimetres), and that the earth is a planet four centuries ago (0.4 millimetres). Napoleon lived 0.2 millimetres ago and Hitler lived 0.07 millimetres ago.

If we count in generations rather than centuries, the brevity of the existence of Homo sapiens and human culture becomes even clearer. If we work on the basis that there are four generations per century, the first signs of culture emerged 400 generations ago, the first pyramids were built 200 generations ago, Julius Caesar lived 80 generations ago and Charlemagne ruled as the Holy Roman Emperor 48 generations ago. People realised that the earth is round 20 generations ago and started to develop modern science 16 generations ago. The industrial revolution began ten generations ago and the Second World War was fought two generations ago.

Seen against the backdrop of millions years of human existence, as a stage of evolution the phenomenon of culture has only recently matured, while science is still a headstrong adolescent. Given that this is the case, is it any wonder that humans are still exhibiting traits of the animal existence they emerged from 400 generations ago? In fact, humans have yet to emerge from the Animalium in many respects. Their lives are still a struggle, and sometimes a grim dog-eat-dog struggle.

Humankind's struggle to exist and survive is still partly a battle against nature in that they have to wrest food and oth-

Humans have only recently arrived on the scene.
Human culture is still in its infancy!

Solidification of the surface of the Earth. Formation of the Earth's geosphere.	47,000,000 centuries ago
The first forms of life appear on Earth. Formation of the Earth's biosphere.	35,000,000 centuries ago
Rudimentary mental functioning starts to develop. Formation of the Earth's psychosphere. (Lack of research data.)	1,000,000 centuries ago?
First signs of hominid existence. Start of the ANIMALIUM.	35,000 centuries ago
First signs of human existence.	2,000 centuries ago
Start of the TRANSITIUM.	100 centuries ago
Start of the current cultural crisis.	1 century ago
People need to understand that only they can save the planet and human culture. They also need to understand that this historic task can only be accomplished by a united humanity. When will we see the start of the HUMANIUM?	Today

er resources from nature. But during the Animalium humans were also engaged in an equally arduous battle among themselves: an ongoing and ruthless battle to survive by being more powerful than the rest. This is why the hallmark of our existing culture is still the need to wage war – on all fronts.

Those who realise how little our existing culture has advanced along the road towards becoming truly human are aware that the development of a humane society promises to be a formidable task.

In other words, seen from the viewpoint of cultural science humankind, as it exists today, is still primitive. Human beings lack humanity.

Human beings are on the way to becoming more human. But the Humanium has yet to appear on the horizon.

6

A look at our primitive horde mentality

Dear Contemporaries,

I do not accept the widespread notion that no society can exist without ongoing struggle, and violent struggle at that. In my view it is entirely unnecessary for us to turn our society into a horror film. But I understand the need for struggle. Our culture is primitive. Being engaged in permanent struggle is one of the characteristics of a primitive society.

Yes, we remain true to this tradition, which dates back to the Animalium. We are not taught this at school, but let us be under no illusion. Human beings lived as animals for hundreds of thousands of years. They were one animal species among others. Like other animals they obtained their food by hunting prey and foraging for what was edible in nature.

In the jungle there is a simple law: kill or be killed. The only way for humans to survive in the jungle was by forming tight-knit groups or hordes. All men learned to defend themselves against natural predators, such as lions, wolves and bears. The human hordes roamed with herds of wild cattle, sheep, horses and deer. Meat was an important food, more important than wild fruit, roots and other edible plant matter. Humans lived mainly on meat. But the hunt was not always successful, and then the members of the horde went hungry.

Animals are either predators or prey. Prey animals live together in large herds, while predators live together in small packs. Which category does the human horde fall into?

Human hordes exhibited many of the characteristics of a herd. The members of the horde were unanimous in their obedience to the command of the leader of the horde. Tight-knit cooperation is essential in the jungle. But humans also behaved like predators, because they had remarkable self-devised and self-built weapons. With their artefacts, artificial weapons and tools, humans mastered the art of survival.

Yet their success at surviving eventually posed its own problems. As the human species grew in number food became increasingly scarce. This meant that as well as defending themselves against predators, humans were also engaged in a life and death battle against the members of other hordes for the possession of hunting grounds.

In other words, humans learnt at a young age from the members of their own horde that the members of other hordes were their enemies. The perpetual state of war meant that the leader of the horde insisted on rigid discipline and absolute obedience. The leader of the horde was the strongest man in the pack. He wielded power over all of the men *and* all of the women. In the horde power was based on superior physical strength. This was accepted without question by the other members of the horde. They belonged to the horde body and soul because the horde was their only means of safety and protection. They entrusted their lives to their leader and, if necessary, they were prepared to give their lives to ensure the survival of the horde.

Has the horde mentality disappeared? No. Leaders are still required to command respect. People are still prepared to take up arms to defend their community. And, if necessary, people are prepared to sacrifice their lives for the sake of the community. Nowadays the community could be anything: a sect, a group of religious fanatics, a group of guerrilla fighters – but more often than not it is the community of one's homeland. In the words of the Dutch national anthem: 'Loyal to the fatherland I will remain until I die!'

In this respect we are still as primitive as we were during the Animalium.

7

From horde mentality to nationalistic mentality

Dear Contemporaries,

The hordes of hundreds of thousands years ago are now known as nations. I myself experienced how boys and men were prepared to do anything for their people. They sacrificed their lives without hesitation. This essentially means that they sacrificed their lives for their national leader. It made no difference whether they were German or Russian or English or French. They were all brought up to regard people of other nations as their enemies. And what do we do with an enemy? We destroy them, we exterminate them, we throttle them, we gas them... The horde mentality is clearly alive and kicking. Today we call it nationalism.

In my younger years I was most disturbed by the way the Germans behaved in this respect. They sang 'Deutschland, Deutschland, über alles, über alles in der Welt!' at the tops of their voices and revered the leader of their horde as a demigod. Since the fall of Nazi Germany at the end of the Second World War the Germans now only sing the third verse of the Deutschlandlied as their national anthem. (The third verse speaks of unity and justice, rather than global supremacy.)

The French continue to sing their national anthem despite the fact that the lyrics outdo all other anthems in their expression of hate against 'others'. The first verse sets the tone: 'Fearsome soldiers are coming into your midst to cut the throats of your sons and consorts.' The second verse announces that a barbarian horde ruled by traitors and conspiratorial kings is planning to return the French to the slavery of antiquity. The remaining verses continue along the same lines. The message to the listener is clear: if you are a foreigner, you are a barbarian. So there is only one thing for it!

If you don't want to go through life as a barbarian, you have to get hold of a French passport. You should be able to find one on the black market.

As well as forming organically through conflict with an enemy, nations are also actively created. Take America for example. The first European settlers largely wiped out the indigenous North American population. Many African people travelled to America on ships, but they did not come of their own accord. They were imported by white people as slaves. Later hundreds of thousands Europeans emigrated to the United States. In the twentieth century people from Mexico, Central America, Asia and Korea in particular were added to the mix. This resulted in a very diverse collection of ethnic groups. The government realised that the members of such a mixed population would not automatically form a nation. So what did the people in government do? They forged the diverse ethnic groups together. They roused nationalistic sentiment through education. A national flag was hung in every school. All newcomers had to learn to speak English. For a long time the descendents of the people imported from Africa were excluded from the national community and treated as second-class citizens. But since Martin Luther King took up their cause they too are treated as real Americans – well, more or less. And they too have become nationalists.

In Europe there was no need to drum up nationalistic sentiment. The French and the Germans had always been sworn enemies, so it went without saying that these countries were nationalistic. But during the course of the 19th century the spirit of nationalism grew among other European peoples. Each country chose a national flag and a national anthem. School children were taught about the national heroes of the past. Compulsory military service was introduced and the young man who joined the army were instilled with an even greater sense of patriotism. Countries erected monuments to their monarchs and revered national figures.

Nationalism is a love of one's country. It is essentially a form of idealism. But all of the wars fought in Europe since the 19th century would never have been possible if the people had told their leaders to fight the wars themselves! While horde mentality can be elevated to the level of idealism, I, for one, would prefer to see humanity liberated from its original horde mentality.

Yet it would seem that we derive a perverse sense of satisfaction from being primitive.

8

Make sure you are more powerful than the rest

Dear Contemporaries,

Just ten thousand years ago human hordes fought over hunting grounds. Those days have gone: human hordes have since evolved into nations of all sizes. But from time to time grim-faced statesmen still call their people to battle like the leaders of the hordes.

Of course, wars are no longer fought over hunting grounds. When human hordes roamed the land the earth had yet to see the advent of industry, which keeps growing and growing and has to be fed with resources such as oil, gas, coal, wood and water, as well as minerals, such as iron, copper, nickel, zinc, aluminium, diamonds, you name it. Yet the deposits of resources in the earth's crust are limited. And the fact that certain nations (and sometimes small ones) have huge oil reserves, or a wealth of other mineral resources, while others have very few mineral deposits if any, is a source of discord.

Nowadays poor countries are busy trying to achieve affluence by taking over the Western economic order. Take China for example. The country has experienced tremendous industrial growth in recent decades and this growth has occurred at an unprecedented rate. The country has almost no natural resources in the ground. So what are the Chinese doing? They are helping poor countries, primarily in Africa, to build a modern economy in exchange for a large share of their resources, for African countries have an abundance of natural resources.

Mineral resources and drinking water are becoming a problem. If all countries industrialise there will be a global shortage of minerals and other resources. In fact, we are witnessing a global war in the making. For it is safe to assume that rich nations will never consent to share their wealth with other countries.

The battle for resources has been underway on a regional scale for some time. America has fought two wars to gain access to the vast oil reserves in Iraq. The second war was said to have the 'noble purpose' of toppling a dangerous and brutal dictator – with a view to installing a compliant government I might add. Central Asia also has substantial oil reserves. This is another region in which Western troops have been deployed, supposedly for the sole purpose of defeating Islamic terrorists. But petroleum is almost certainly a significant factor behind the scenes of this military action. The whole world is gradually becoming a stage on which the battle for resources is being fought out.

As any close observer of this power game will know, governments, diplomats and spies are not the only ones involved. Armed forces are also playing a significant role. Sometimes military generals stage a coup. When they do it becomes clear that military leaders who take on the role of statesmen are particularly inhumane. The reign of terror wielded in Chile by General Pinochet, in Argentina by Commander Videla (approximately 30,000 dissenters 'disappeared' while he was in power), in China first by Chiang Kai Shek and then by his opponent Mao Zedong, and in Africa by Idi Amin ('the butcher of Africa') are all notorious examples.

Why do armed forces play such a significant role in world politics? The answer is obvious. There is no power without weapons. There is often a colossal war industry in powerful countries. Hundreds of billions are spent on the manufacture of weapons and arms deals. And modern weapons are not just canons, machine guns, bombs, grenades, tanks, warships, aircraft, drones, missiles and nuclear weapons. Countries are now rapidly developing chemical and biological weapons too.

Those who possess power usually find the power game fascinating. They enjoy it. And there are reasons why. It appeals to the feelings that predominated during the Animalium. Or, to be more precise, feelings that date back to the days when humans lived as an animal among animals and had yet to be troubled by human feelings.

How gratifyingly primitive!

9

We put our faith in the nuclear bomb

Dear Contemporaries,

American military capacity is formidable - the US defence budget now represents nearly half of all global military expenditure. It is a professional military machine that consists of highly advanced weapons systems, including a large arsenal of long-range missiles and nuclear weapons.

The United States is clearly the most powerful superpower of our time. It is an immense empire that dwarfs the earlier Roman Empire and it wields its power and influence over the whole world. Nevertheless, it now finds itself confronted with competitors in the battle for global supremacy.

The leading superpowers of our day are engaged in a concerted effort to increase their military strength. The five victors of the Second World War (the United States, Russia, the United Kingdom, China and France) are the only nations officially recognized as states permitted to develop nuclear weapons. This was agreed in the so-called Treaty on the Non-Proliferation of Nuclear Weapons, which was signed from 1968 onwards by all countries of significance with the exception of Israel. All 'non-nuclear-weapon states' that are party to the treaty agree to refrain from nuclear armament. However, the enrichment of uran ium is permitted.

Despite the impressive-sounding wording of the treaty, which speaks of the commitment to nuclear disarmament, the practice of world politics basically involves threatening to attack opponents with superior military power, particularly and preferably nuclear weapons. This approach is contagious. Several non-parties to the treaty are known or believed to have developed their own nuclear weapons. India and Pakistan openly admit that they have nuclear weapon capabilities. Israel has never admitted to having nuclear weapons but is widely believed to have nuclear capability. North Korea is conducting nuclear tests and Iran is thought to be developing nuclear weapons. From a technological point of view there is nothing to stop many countries producing nuclear bombs given that the enrichment of uranium is not prohibited. There are currently thought to be just under 40,000 nuclear weapons in the world. We can but hope that they are never used.

You might be inclined to say, "Ah but Mr Steenis, being engaged in a struggle is part and parcel of human existence. You yourself have told us that this has always been the case. Take it from me, Mr Steenis, it will always be the case. It's lovely that you are such a peace-loving person, but you shouldn't waste your time on pacifism."

If you take this view, I would point out that you are choosing to remain passive in the face of an impending Third World War – a war that will inevitably be fought with nuclear weapons. Have you ever considered what that would mean for the human race? It's quite simple: it would mean the end of the human race. If you are not prepared to accept that, you might like to acquaint yourself with what happened in Hiroshima in 1945. And bear in mind that the atomic bomb the Americans dropped on Hiroshima was relatively small. Today's nuclear bombs are vastly more powerful!

Humankind's technological capabilities have advanced at an exponential rate – yet while this has been happening the global community has remained primitive in many respects. What we have to ask ourselves is whether virtually unlimited technological capability and a primitive global community of power-hungry states is a good combination. I'm afraid that the answer is no.

We invest tremendous energy in the development of technology. And there is nothing wrong with that. But it seems to me that it is imperative that we first need to everything in our power to prevent a nuclear war. I realise that this is easier said than done. In opposing the established order with its thirst for power and domination we will find ourselves in conflict with enormous established interests.

But surely the continued existence of humankind is more important.

10

The perpetual need to engage in battle

Dear Contemporaries,

Apart from its impressive technological development, human society is still very primitive in many respects. What can we do about this? I often hear the argument that there's no point thinking we can do something about it. Society cannot be repaired. Dictators such as Hitler, Stalin and Mao Zedong were all trying to 'improve' society. Well, thank you very much, but no thank you! And I agree: that's certainly not the way to go about it!

These days it's fashionable to talk about 'giving social forces free rein', leaving plenty of room for competition. Free enterprise will bring prosperity and affluence. No need for government interference. Freedom is the highest principle!

But therein lies the rub. If we welcome a hands-off government that refrains from intervening, it essentially means that we end up doing nothing about the primitiveness of our society. So society remains stage on which we engage in endless battle on all fronts.

If businesses compete with each other in a free economy, they are basically doing battle with each other – albeit not with weapons, but still. We glorify competition. In other words, all businesses fight to survive and to continue to exist. Where have I heard that before? Precisely! That's what happens in nature, where there is one cardinal rule: kill or be killed.

Modern-day society is still fighting the battle that was unavoidable during the Animalium: the battle against nature, that is. And we appear to be winning: we are systematically destroying nature. We are also doing battle among ourselves. Just as in the past hordes would wipe out rival hordes, in the modern era each new World War shows how effective we have become at applying the old cardinal rule: kill or be killed.

The catchphrase of our time is 'freedom for the entrepreneur'. And it is a catchphrase that is spreading. It is essentially an injunction to 'live in accordance with the rule of nature'. Or to continue to engage in a modern-day version of the battle that characterises the Animalium.

And, although it is never openly acknowledged, the same approach is adopted in politics. The leading figures in each party endeavour to make life impossible for each other, within the bounds of what is legally permitted of course. On a larger scale there are battles between one nation and another and between a nation and its people. New armed conflict can break out at any moment – which happens to be very convenient for the weapons industry by the way. In this arena too we remain loyal to the cardinal rule of the Animalium: kill or be killed. Jews were all but wiped out in Europe not long ago, and similar acts of genocide, the mass slaughter of fellow human beings, have, more recently, been pursued on other continents, much like a new sport.

Speaking of sport, the horde mentality is demonstrated in all its glory in football stadiums, where anything goes, as long as it doesn't result in a red card. Supporters in the stands roar and whistle when the other team has possession of the ball. For the other team is of course the enemy. In 1940 the German army invaded the Netherlands. The small country held out for five days before capitulating after the Luftwaffe bombed the centre of Rotterdam. From then on the Dutch harboured a deep-rooted resentment against the Germans, which was only dispelled when Dutch beat the Germans at football. National honour had been restored.

The delirious delight expressed by fans when their side

wins comes across as very primitive. The members of a horde would almost certainly have expressed similar jubilation during the Animalium after successfully wiping out an enemy horde. Sport is battle - and battle is sport. The popularity of kickboxing and other martial arts speaks for itself.

11

Advanced material culture is not the be all and end all

Dear Contemporaries,

The principle of non-intervention in the social, economic and financial order, supposedly in the interest of freedom, leads to crises. Many people have come to realise that this is the case. Things are initiated without being properly coordinated. Non-intervention means that nothing is done about the vast differences between rich and poor. Or about the fact that the earth's crust is being plundered. Or that our tropical rainforests are being destroyed – so the land they once occupied will eventually turn into a desert. Or that species are dying out on a daily basis. If there hadn't been some sort of intervention, there would no longer be any whales in the oceans. The atmosphere would contain higher concentrations of contaminants left by emissions of industrial gases. And the water in our rivers, lakes and seas would be more heavily polluted than is now often the case.

By refraining from intervening, by doing nothing, we are essentially choosing to walk off the edge of the cliff with our eyes wide open. Let us reflect deeply on the mistakes we are making mistakes that threaten the future of the generations that will come after us. Let us stop and ask ourselves how it is that a race capable of achieving such rapid technological advancement is failing to evolve into a less primitive society.

In my view reflection is what is lacking. Reflection on changes that are urgently needed.

I say: there needs to be a great revolution. Human beings are capable of more than technological tours de force. I am not calling for a violent revolution, but for a revolution in the mentality of the global population. A revolution that seeks to evolve beyond primitive ways of being, to refine human culture, to ban violence, to maintain world peace and to promote global solidarity. In other words, a revolution that seeks to humanise the global community.

You might feel that this is aiming far too high, that this is idealism divorced from reality – inspiring daydreams but ultimately utopian daydreams. In response to which I would say, yes, of course the revolution I am describing is a distant prospect, but the awareness that change is needed is growing. What will it take for us to wake up and take action?

For it is important not to underestimate the human race. Homo sapiens is a remarkably successful phenomenon. No other animal species has come close to achieving what humankind has achieved. In our lifetime, human beings have become masters of the earth. They have left their mark on the entire surface of the globe. They determine what grows where. Forests have given way to meadows and fields, orchards and plantations. Cities have sprung up everywhere, often with millions of inhabitants. Buildings that rise sky-high are a testament to the triumph of humankind. There are schools, libraries, concert halls, museums, stadiums, sports complexes, office complexes and extensive industrial estates. There are also aerial transmitters, motorways and dual carriageways, inland waterways, seaports and airports.

Of course this is really just one aspect of culture - material culture. Human beings alter the natural environment and replace nature with culture. So this is all about material things. And, when it comes to material things, success has already been achieved. But then of course there are also the immaterial aspects of culture.

And these aspects lag far behind technological progress. The progress that is now needed is the progress that will be inspired by man's reflection on his inner life and his social behaviour.

To solve the problems of the global community we need humanity, and humanity is always synonymous with human solidarity.

12

Isn't being truly human something worth striving for?

Dear Contemporaries,

The arrival of culture and the attendant changes in the surrounding natural and social environment led to changes in man's inner life. There is a vast difference between the life of a farmer and town-dweller and life as a member of a horde. We have now evolved beyond that stage of our existence and have left behind us life as an animal among animals. We now live as human beings together with our fellow human beings.

The evolution of man's inner life can be described as a process of humanisation: the process of becoming truly human. Humans become different from animals in every respect. I believe it is correct to say that there are people, and there are animals. How have humans and animals differed since the arrival of culture?

Humans have always been more intelligent than animals. It is their intelligence that fuels the quest for knowledge and insight. But human emotions - human nature in a narrower sense - are also typically human. Human nature expresses itself through attitudes such as responsibility, helpfulness, compassion, respect for others and solidarity. Let's look at these two things: the quest for knowledge on the one hand and the spirit of human solidarity on the other.

As far as the quest for knowledge is concerned, for centuries prophets and priests have sought to provide answers to the fundamental questions of human existence. Their answers all agree that the divine is a mystery: there is a power above us to which we can only surrender.

These days we also have scientists. Many of them offer different answers to these questions. They claim that nature and all aspects of reality can be explained. One of our tasks as human beings is to seek knowledge and understanding of the world that surrounds us. In principle, human beings are capable of fathoming the whole of existence.

As a broad generalisation, I agree with the latter view. But I would qualify this by saying that we would do well to understand that science is still in its infancy. Man may possess sufficient knowledge of nature to take technology to impressive heights, but scientists are no more capable of providing answers to the fundamental questions regarding the nature of reality than mystics. And when it comes to society and culture – well, this is clearly a sphere of which we have very little understanding. This is one of the reasons why our society is such a shambles. Without an understanding of the phenomenon of culture, it will be impossible for us to put an end to the current chaos, the perpetual battle, the violence, the atrocities and the barbarity.

I think the worst thing about all of this is that people do not realise that man's destiny is to become truly human and that society should be organized in a way that will facilitate this. Yet you won't find any mention of the humanisation of society in any of the national constitutions. They prohibit all kinds of things that are thought to be unacceptable. But what, if anything, is being done to make people more humane?

The current education system is failing miserably in this respect. The purpose of education is always said to be the impartation of knowledge – together with the skills needed to apply this knowledge. I have to admit that, in this respect, the current education system achieves what it sets out to do. The poisonous gas used to exterminate millions of Jews and Romani people in the twentieth century was undoubtedly manufactured by people who had received a good education. The gas they produced was very effective.

It is often said that many countries have an excellent education system.

But aren't our education systems missing the point?

13

We are experiencing an ongoing and profound cultural crisis

Dear Contemporaries,

It is clear to those who study the phenomenon of culture from a distance that during the course of ten thousand years of cultural development there have been various stages of flowering punctuated by periods of crisis.

In Europe, for example, the transition from the Middle Ages to the modern era was marked by a period of cultural crisis. There were uprisings, wars, religious dissent, piracy, persecution of heresy, moral decay, occultism, cruelty and barbarity, inflation and impoverishment of the once powerful nobility. At the same time there were also natural disasters such as plagues and floods. These were centuries of despair and loss of established values and traditions.

Yet out of the chaos emerged renewal. People built nations on new foundations. They also built ocean-going vessels that could sail the seas, discovered sea routes and invented all kinds of things, including the art of book printing. An affluent middle class arose, there was religious reform, the foundations of modern science began to take shape, there was an unprecedented flowering of the arts, the first foreign colonies were founded by Europeans, trade was more profitable than ever before, there were new forms of industry, and the growth of economic prosperity was facilitated partly by the new phenomenon of banking.

It is easy to see the parallels between the period of crisis that preceded the modern era and what we are currently experiencing. There are obvious similarities, such as the prevalence of conflict and violence – and simultaneous advances in knowledge and technology, which are happening so fast that we can barely keep up with them.

But here I would like to focus on the differences. The transition from the Middle Ages to the modern era was a stage in the cultural evolution of Europe. The crisis we are experiencing today is not simply a European affair. European culture has spread throughout the world at an exponential rate. There is now a global culture. Modern cities are the same wherever you go, the same muzak is played in the stores, the same magazine programmes, soaps, interviews and formulaic entertainment are shown on television – the only thing that differs is the language. Even so, you can generally get by with English, from Shanghai to Rio de Janeiro and from Stavanger to Cape Town. Retail outlets in shopping centres sell the same clothes in the same fabrics in similar, if not identical, designs. The media report the same world news, and the prices of goods, services and foods follow world market prices.

These days a local economic recession spreads from region to region and from continent to continent. The current recession appears to be making itself felt throughout the world. This makes it clear that humanity will have to unite in order to be able to take decisive action in response to crises.

There is also another lesson: there was a single overriding factor that enabled Europe to overcome the cultural crisis that ushered out the Middle Ages and ushered in the modern era. And that was a revolution in the thinking of the day, a new attitude toward the world, a new vision of the world. This was what gave birth to modern science. It then rapidly became clear that modern science would pave a way to the future.

As twenty-first century humans undergo an increasingly serious cultural crisis, we too need a new mentality and a new worldview. Modern thinking needs to give way to a new kind of thinking and a new vision.

Modern thinking - a station we have passed

14

The constant quest for certainty

Dear Contemporaries,

We cannot improve society as things stand. At the moment our understanding of society falls short because our understanding of the phenomenon of man falls short. To create a better society, first we need to gain a deeper understanding of man's inner world. The scientific discipline that studies mental function and behaviour – psychology – fails in this respect. And we might question whether psychology is the only branch of science that fails to arrive at adequate understanding.

Ladies and Gentlemen of science, before you rush to protest, bear in mind that all aspects of science are barely out of the cradle. They are still in their primitive early stages. And is that so surprising? If human society as a whole is still primitive, surely the same is bound to apply to our current science. Admittedly, we have achieved tremendous technological advancement, but from the point of view of cultural science, we have made very little progress. Man is a mystery to himself.

There is something fundamentally wrong with our way of thinking. My view on the matter is this: human existence automatically involves the constant endeavour to make sense of what is happening in the surroundings. Humans have to do this, in order to know how to act. Creatures that live in the jungle have to be hypervigilant every second. Yet that is actually the case everywhere. We are constantly compelled to use our senses, because we have to ascertain what is going on around us. In other words, the first function of thinking is always to ascertain what is going on.

At this point you might be thinking, "We already know this, Mr Steenis. When are you going to tell us something new? But read on. The urge to ascertain what is going on around us is motivated by the desire for certainty. Is this something that can be achieved? Well, in most instances yes. But not when it comes to the deeper questions of human existence. The answers to these questions cannot be ascertained. So, because it is difficult to live with uncertainty, we listen avidly to people who claim to know the way of things.

The priests of old informed those who listened to them that man was dependent on the whims of the gods and that natural disasters were a sign that the gods were displeased. The people had to do something to try to appease the wrath of the gods. How? By making sacrifices. If natural disasters continued to happen, it meant that the sacrifices were too small. It seems the people were slow to realise that they kept having to make greater and greater sacrifices. In some ancient farming cultures mothers had to give their first-born to the priests to be sacrificed. And in ancient Greece farmers were sometimes so desperate that they sacrificed their whole herd. This is where the word 'holocaust' comes from. Yet, despite all of these sacrifices, the people never had any certainty.

So how does one gain certainty? Well, in Europe the Middle Ages were followed by the emergence of modern science. Thinkers in previous centuries tried to establish certainty and failed. The practitioners of modern science managed to find a way to provide certainty. How? They used a growing array of instruments to make systematic observations and carefully noted the results. Then they examined whether it was possible to deduce rules and correlations from the factual data they had compiled. If this was the case, they concluded that they had formulated a theory that accounted for the facts. But how could they prove that the theory was correct?

This is one of the trump cards of modern science. It is possible to prove whether a theory is true or false. Back in antiquity scholars started developing a branch of science that produced certainty, even absolute certainty. They established indisputable basic certainties and then deduced other certainties by logically inferring them from the basic certainties. If you carefully adhere to this principle, in other words, if you always proceed logically, you always remain within the realm of certainty. Here we find ourselves in the domain of mathematics: 'the art of exactness or certainty'.

Modern science adheres to the principle that a theory is true if its accuracy can be mathematically determined. In other words, this is how you establish with certainty that something is the case!

Proof that conforms to the rules of modern science is irrefutable - or so it is claimed.

15

Thinking that seeks to ascertain reality falls short

Dear Contemporaries,

Can we safely assume that a person who has ascertained something and can prove it mathematically will never make an erroneous statement? I'm afraid not. Let me give you an example from my own experience. Long ago, when I was still a boy, there was a radio play series for children. I enjoyed every episode. It was an exciting story about a group of people who travelled to the moon.

One day my brother and I were sitting at home in the kitchen drinking tea with our mother after school. I was still at primary school but my brother was older, so he was in secondary school. My brother told us that one of his classmates had asked the physics teacher whether space travel was possible. The teacher smiled sympathetically and said: "I'm sorry to have to disappoint you my boy, but that kind of things only happens in a radio play or in science fiction. Space travel is impossible." The teacher explained why space travel was out of the question and wrote a few mathematical formulas on the blackboard, which proved that what he was saying was true. "You see," he said. "It's absolutely impossible." I took an instant dislike to the teacher who had said such a thing. But my brother said, "He's right!"

More than thirty years later, in 1969, as I watched Neil Armstrong become the first man to step foot on the moon, I suddenly remembered what the physics teacher had said all those years ago and thought how strange it was that he had somehow been able to provide mathematical proof that space travel was impossible. He knew the facts, he was an expert and he was reporting laws ascertained by science.

And it suddenly dawned on me that the key lay in the

word 'ascertain'. You can only ascertain something with absolute certainty if that something does not change. The physics teacher from my childhood was talking about space travel. But space travel is something that changes and evolves. Something that is not possible today might well be possible tomorrow!

I began to wonder how modern science dealt with dynamic processes such as change and evolution.

The verb 'to ascertain' originally meant 'to make certain': to firmly establish the truth of something that can then be regarded as a certainty. Something that has been firmly established is literally unshakable. Figuratively speaking, it is accepted as unshakably true. A truth that is considered to have been established is thought to be eternally true. Modern scientists subscribe to a worldview that has been firmly established. Reality does not change, they say. Or, to be more precise, this was something they once said. For they have since been forced to admit that there is such a thing as evolution. So what can be ascertained?

The people of modern science do not admit defeat easily. They do not allow the inconvenient fact of evolution to throw a spanner in their carefully ascertained works! They reduce the significance of evolution by claiming that evolution is a phenomenon that only occurs in certain systems, such as life on earth. But it is now apparent that everything that exists is evolving: the whole cosmos is an evolving organism. How is the scholarly community going to reduce the significance of that inconvenient fact? How will they continue to subscribe to their firmly established worldview?

People are prepared to acknowledge that evolution is a process of sequential change. But, they say, these changes are not fundamental or qualitative differences. Evolution never adds something genuinely new. In other words, reality remains essentially the same. The same laws of nature apply throughout the cosmos, matter is always composed of the same particles, energy always manifests in the same forms, and the light that shines is the same light everywhere.

Modern science asserts the principle of the uniformity of nature and maintains that there are no fundamental differences in nature. Nature is homogenous. We can simply keep ascertaining facts and proving them mathematically. That is the only thing that leads to certainty.

Unfortunately for science, this reasoning is not sound as we have seen. A system that is evolving is unascertainable. The assumption that phenomena that are evolving can be reduced to facts that can be ascertained as eternally true is one of the greatest blunders of modern science.

16

Another flaw in the thinking that seeks to ascertain reality

Dear Contemporaries,

We have to abandon the idea of a firmly established and unshakable worldview arrived at through ascertainment. And there is another aspect to the thinking that seeks to ascertain reality that we need to be aware of. When we ascertain something we do not make a distinction between what we ascertain and the thing itself. We constantly use abstractions and then treat them as concrete. To give you an example:

The Monday morning newspaper headline states in big bold print:

Weekend traffic claims victims yet again

There is nothing unusual about this sentence. But what does it actually say? It tells us that traffic is a bloodthirsty brute. Do you see the brute there in front of you? No, of course not! The concept of traffic is an abstraction. We use concepts like this to express ourselves clearly and concisely. And that's fine. But concepts only exist in our mind and intellect. They are not part of the reality that surrounds us. The question is, do we realise this? Our use of language suggests not!

If you pay attention you will come across thousands of examples of this kind of usage. 'Winners overcome by emotion.' 'Financial crisis puts pressure on share prices.' 'The mood was elated.' 'The market share has shrunk.' 'The housing industry is stagnant.' 'Pessimism is growing.' 'The beauty of the landscape is enchanting.' 'The invention of the printing press reduced illiteracy.' 'Price increases reduce revenue growth.' 'Magellan's world voyage proved that the earth was round.' 'The Renaissance produced a flowering of the arts.' 'Parenting has become more conscious'. 'Taxation is a heavy burden on the population.' 'Family life is going through a crisis'. 'The tropical rainforests are shrinking.' 'Society is sick'. 'No matter what the future may bring…' And so on.

We constantly treat concepts and ideas, that is abstractions, as if they were real. Or, to use a more sophisticated term, we reify abstractions.

So we see errors such as, 'Psychological factors played a significant role in the recent election.' The reporter meant to say that mental factors played a role, but people commonly confuse 'psyche' and 'psychology'. A similar thing occurs when people refer to 'biological evolution', which literally means the evolution of biology. What is really being referred to is 'the evolution of life on earth', hence it is accurate to refer to 'biotic evolution'.

To sum up: for centuries people have been reifying their thoughts about reality. In other words, they mistake their thoughts for reality. They invent ideas of demons, spirits, gods and goddesses and then proceed to fear and worship them. They conceive the idea of salvation and live in hope of reward in the hereafter.

Of course, you might say that scientists don't do such a thing. They deliberately make a point of taking their thinking into account.

If only that were true.

17

Reification – the pitfall of modern science

Dear Contemporaries,

In history books you will read that 'the French Revolution caused great turmoil throughout France.' But the actual fact was that there was great turmoil throughout France. That was the reality of the situation. To place the chain of chaotic events that unfolded in a coherent context, historians formulated the concept of the French Revolution, which is an abstraction. Such a concept is necessary to make sense of a period that happened in the past. I call this kind of abstraction a summarising concept. Our reification of the French Revolution means that we present the revolution an entity capable of action. But this is not the case. The persons who took action were the revolutionaries and counter-revolutionaries. Yet historians are often guilty of reifying the concept of revolution. For example, they write that, 'The French Revolution sent shockwaves through Europe.'

Physicists are also quite happy to reify. Certain patterns can be observed in nature. These patterns are said to be the laws of nature. What do physicists do? They reify the concept of the law of nature without thinking about it. They attribute to the abstract laws of nature the ability to play an active role in nature. Seen from the point of view of the physicists, abstract laws of nature determine what happens in nature.

In other words, what people fail to take into account is the following: a summarising concept refers to something concrete or real. These kinds of concepts are closely related to something real. But in order to be able to form an image, people also have to use concepts that do not refer to something concrete or real. I call concepts that are needed to form an image of reality, conceptual constructs. These include abstract notions such as the laws of nature, cause and effect, dimension, and time and space. Their only purpose is to help us form an image of reality.

Science is in great danger when we fall into the trap of reification. When we reify the concept of a 'galactic system', for example, we overlook the enormous diversity in the structures of different galactic systems. We do the same thing when we reify the concept of a 'tree'. But these summarising concepts do at least refer to concrete things. When we reify conceptual constructs we make an error of a different order. Allow me to explain why.

Time and space are conceptual constructs. Time is a convention that helps the human mind determine whether certain events took place before or after other events, and space is a vast nothing, the dialectic opposite of something. Time and space do not have any physical properties. But this is precisely the assumption made by physicists.

They attribute physical properties to the concept of time. In fact, piles of volumes have been written about the properties of the concept of time. How do the authors pull that off! All that is missing is a novel in which time is the main protagonist.

Over the centuries the process of reification has led people to depict time as an old man. Physicists can even tell us precisely when he was born. His birth coincided with the Big Bang. There is no record of Mother Nature sending birth announcements. But it would have been difficult, given that her birth also coincided with the Big Bang. Prior to that there was nothing – or so the physicists tell us with great conviction.

But, in referring to the birth of time, the physicists inadvertently reveal their belief in the creation of the universe. For if there was nothing before the Big Bang, then what caused the Big Bang? Surely there must have been a prior Creator? The Big Bang theory, in this form, is essentially a creation myth in a modern scientific guise.

Yet cosmologists and other physicists never speak out

against it, because they have mathematics, 'the art of certainty', on their side. Their picture of reality is based on mathematical formulas. They have no qualms about using summarising concepts and conceptual constructs interchangeably in their mathematical descriptions of reality. Their formulas are a mishmash of references: some point to reality and others point to pictures of and ideas about reality.

But then, the way they see it, the products of their abstract mathematical approach remain valid for all eternity.

18

Einstein: reifying in four dimensions

Dear Contemporaries,

So now you know: the whole of nature is depicted with mathematical formulas – in other words reified formulas. If you are good at mathematics, you will automatically be good at natural science, especially physics!

This was amply demonstrated by Einstein, who was a great mathematician. Until Einstein arrived on the scene mathematicians had always maintained that space had three dimensions, namely length, width and height. This applied to everything that occupied space, in other words it applied to all objects.

But Einstein thought, "Objects don't only exist in space, they also exist in time. At zero time nothing exists. To describe reality we need both spatial dimensions and time. So it would be better to include time as a fourth, spatial dimension. It would be better to picture reality as a four-dimensional space-time continuum."

Having come to this conclusion, Einstein went on to design a four-dimensional image of the cosmos. Yet is it appropriate to use the word 'image' in this context? No, not really, because very few people can conceive of a four-dimensional space-time continuum. It seems to me that Einstein's 'spacetime' can only lead a mathematical existence. Reification of this kind of mathematical model would result in the creation of a very remarkable reality!

As far as the reification of space is concerned, as a lay person I assumed that cosmic space was a vast nothing, and that the reification of nothing is also bound to be nothing. Yet in Einstein's thinking nothing could be further from the truth! He saw space as a physical reality and – or so I am led to believe – he even described space as curved! When I read this it makes my toes curl.

Einstein also reified time and introduced the notion that time could speed up and slow down depending on how fast something is moving. If an object is moving at a speed that approaches the speed of light, the speed of time approaches zero. In other words, a photon - a particle of light - can travel through the whole universe in zero time! If this is the case, I have a tip for those among us who enjoy life: work out how to attain the speed of light and you will live forever! You will stop growing older!

You might well feel the need to respond to this critique. Indeed, you might be inclined to say, "Mr Steenis, you are clearly not an expert. You are simply concocting a specious line of reasoning to make Einstein and physics look ridiculous. Do you really think that this is the kind of critique we have been waiting for?"

I understand why you would adopt such a view, gentlemen of physics. Feel free to keep ascertaining and reifying by all means. But, while you're at it, you might want to put a sign above the entrance to your scientific institute that says in big bold lettering:

LONG LIVE PRIMITIVENESS!

19

EINSTEIN - A MODERN FAIRY TALE

Dear Contemporaries,

Einstein was particularly preoccupied with the problem presented by the often unexpected and not immediately explicable motions observed in the heavens.

The motions observed in the heavens had always presented a problem. From the dawn of ages humans wanted to orient themselves in the wide world that surrounded them. Even thousands of years ago people watched the movements of the celestial bodies.

If you observe celestial bodies you see remarkable phenomena, such as the orbits of the planets. In fact, planets came to be defined by their orbits, for the word 'planet' means 'wandering star'. Planets behave very differently from fixed stars. Fixed stars maintain in the same position relative to each other and form constellations, in which ancient stargazers imagined they could see all kinds of creatures. But planets sometimes appear to temporarily reverse their direction of motion as they move through the heavens!

The ancient Greek scholar, Ptolemy, came up with an ingenious theory that would account for the anomalous motions of the planets. He suggested that the universe was made up of a series of spheres. Each of these spheres has its own motion. The fixed stars, the sun, the moon and all of the planets all move within separate spheres. However, what Ptolemy failed to realise was that he was making the unconscious assumption that the earth was the centre of the universe.

Ptolemy's worldview endured for fourteen centuries. And indeed, this geocentric model made it possible to account for many of the movements of celestial bodies, albeit with the aid of a complex system of cycles and hundreds of 'epicycles'.

Nicolaus Copernicus proposed an alternative solution which ushered in the era of modern science. He mentally positioned himself outside the movements of the sun and planets. When the respective motions were viewed from a distance, things fell into place and the answer became clear: the sun is at the centre and each planet follows its own orbit around the sun. The perspective of a heliocentric system reveals that the earth is also a planet and that, viewed from the earth, planets with orbits larger than that of the earth appear

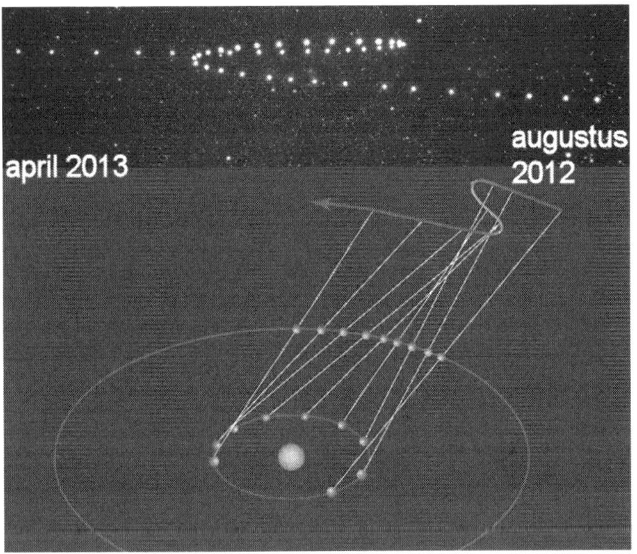

Copernicus was on the right track. But he assumed that the perfection of God's creation meant that the orbits of the planets were bound to be perfectly circular. His observations revealed that this was not the case.
The process of scientific research begins with the formulation of a hypothesis.
If the facts do not support this initial presumption, the scientist has to be prepared to abandon the hypothesis. But Copernicus did not abandon his hypothesis. Like Ptolemy before him, he went back to the idea of cycles and epicycles. This led him away from greater understanding!
Modern scientists base their research on the assumption that the universe is evolving. The underlying hypothesis proposes that the process of evolution does not result in the emergence of essential, qualitative differences.
The question is, do the facts support this presumption?

to temporarily reverse their direction of motion.

In other words, drawing conclusions from observations is a complex process. Since everything in the universe is moving, what we observe differs depending on where we are and how we are moving. Or, to put it another way, all observations are relative. Galileo understood this.

We have since understood that the universe contains a lot more than our little solar system. The sun is just one of an enormous cloud of stars, a star system of hundreds of millions stars. And the bewildering enormity of the cosmos doesn't end there, for the universe is filled with millions of these star systems.

From the start, the human quest for knowledge was driven by the need to gain a sense of orientation in relation to the surrounding reality. We now know that the universe is indescribably vast. But we are still left wondering about our location in the universe.

Cosmologists try to explain how the universe was formed. The prevailing assumption is that cosmic matter was originally in a highly compressed state and that, billions of years ago, there was a primordial explosion that caused the dense cosmic matter to expand. How has the structure of the universe evolved over time?

Einstein's mathematical model makes it difficult to answer this question. Copernicus was only able to form a more accurate image of the solar system when he mentally positioned himself outside the movements of the sun and planets. Observing from inside the system led people to the wrong conclusions.

However, rather than mentally positioning himself outside the system, like Copernicus before him, Einstein continued to envisage cosmic space as seen from the earth. He tried to explain his observations with his theory of relativity based on four dimensions of space. And, with his new mathematical model, he appeared to succeed.

But a coherent vision of the workings of the cosmos faded from view. From the earth we see a vast array of star systems, almost all of which appear to be moving away from us. But the workings of the universe as a whole are an inextricable whirl. The question is, what is the structure of the whole? We do not have an answer. But that is hardly surprising.

Einstein's theory of four dimensions forms an insurmountable stumbling block. This is because - wait for it – a four-dimensional spacetime continuum does not have a centre! Or, to put it another way, the centre is everywhere!

And, dear reader, I am sure you will agree that the answer Einstein came up with is crystal clear. Mathematicians understand it immediately. Surely you do too reader? What's that? You don't understand it? Well, let me tell you, I don't understand it any more than you do. That must mean that we are both intellectually incapable!

Or maybe not! In the previous letter I suggested that, on reflection, the theory of four-dimensionality leads to absurd notions. The idea that a photon can travel through the whole universe in no time! The idea that if you attain the speed of light you will live forever!

Among the ranks of modern physicists, surely there must be some who see how absurd this is, just like you and I. Surely they feel compelled to offer a critique whenever the opportunity presents itself. Yet, no matter how carefully I listen, I can't hear anything.

What is going on? Why can't I hear anything?

I think I can explain why. Over time Einstein's enormous fame led him to be hailed as a superhuman genius. He was perceived as an almost mythical emperor. As such he was able to create magical clothes out of conceptual fabrics. And he wore his new clothes with such elegance that his palace servants followed his example. They remain loyal to his magical wardrobe to this day. Yet, I can't help but wonder whether they are simply oblivious to the rules of common decency that tell us not to wander around naked in public.

In primitive societies fairy tales are popular surrogates for reality. Scholars who proclaim these fairy tales can go on to become world famous. When I was young there were scholars who presented strictly scientific evidence in support of their theory that there were inferior and superior races.

Their greatest supporters were genocide perpetrators. Genocide is frowned upon these days. It is thought to be in very bad taste. I couldn't agree more. So their fairy tales are no longer popular. But, as we have seen, other fairy tales are still very much alive in the corridors of modern science.

It seems we modern humans can't do without fairy tales. Believing in fairy tales is far more palatable than facing the harsh reality.

Such as the harsh reality that there will come a time when we cease to exist.

And the even harsher reality that, if we continue as we are, humankind will soon cease to exist.

20

Einstein - a tragic life

Dear Contemporaries,

Einstein played a major role on the world stage. He was 35 years old when the First World War broke out and 60 when the Second World War began. During the First World War he was an active pacifist. The police actually kept an eye on him. Yet when the Second World War broke out he was instrumental in facilitating the production of the atomic bomb.

The man who was such a master of logical reasoning failed to instigate a rational worldview and also failed to contribute to the emergence of a rational society.

Einstein based his reasoning on formal logic, the logic of mathematics. This accounts for his success as a mathematician – and his failure as a physicist. Nature is an evolving organism and, as such, it does not conform to the laws of formal logic. And the same is equally true of an evolving society.

Since 1900 there have been signs of a change in the prevailing thinking. Einstein can be seen as one of the brilliant intellectuals who contributed to the revolution in modern thought. His thinking on relativity represented a breakthrough in theoretical physics. But he and other physicists of his day who ushered in new ideas continued to rely on the same old thinking that seeks to ascertain reality, which inevitably involves reification.

Einstein fled from Germany to escape the Nazis and settled in America. He fled from irrationality. He especially hated the irrational antisemitism by which he too felt threatened. He continued to practice logic, as he understood it, more assiduously than ever before. His mathematical abilities put him at the forefront of those who understood the potential energy stored in the atom - and how that energy could be released. Many scientists wondered whether this would enrich civilization. Well, yes, Gentlemen! If you believe that civilization is enriched by the enrichment of uranium.

This was why, in 1939, Einstein wrote to President Roosevelt of the United States and urged him to build an atomic bomb before the Nazis did. When Roosevelt did not reply, Einstein wrote to him again the following year and this time his letter had the desired result. The first atomic bomb was developed in Los Alamos under the leadership of an American general. Einstein was deliberately excluded from the project because of his pacifist sentiments. But in 1945 the task was complete and two atomic bombs were ready for use. Einstein had shown the world the way. He was the herald of the atomic age.

And then Einstein, a committed pacifist, looked on as American armed forces proceeded to drop two atomic bombs on Japan. He considered the deaths of many tens of thousands of civilians to be both irrational and unnecessary. As far as he was concerned, simply threatening to use the bombs would have been enough.

How tragic for this gifted man that the new worldview he proposed impeded rather than enabled the discovery of the structure of the universe. How tragic that he failed to free himself from the thinking that seeks to ascertain reality, with its inevitable reification and adherence to formal logic. Even more tragic was his failure as a man of peace. And this is doubly tragic when we bear in mind that he conceived of the establishment of supranational authority that would have the right and the power to put a stop to warmongering. So Einstein's life reflects the cultural crisis we are currently experiencing in that it combines confusion and regression with attempts at renewal - attempts that have yet to lead to a fundamental change, a new era and a new stage in human culture.

21

What might the cosmos look like?

Dear Contemporaries,

To my way of thinking, space without a centre is an absurd notion. In fact, as far as I am concerned, space without a centre is not only inconceivable but also impossible. And, I'm sure that you, the reader, think this too. For if we reify the concept of space without a centre, a purely mathematical construct, as physicists persist in doing, it implies that the cosmos does not have a centre!

It seems to me that, if there was a primordial explosion, surely the epicentre of the explosion must be the centre of the universe! But apparently astronomers do not seek to find the centre because they are convinced that it does not exist! Einstein, the emperor of modern thinking about the cosmos, established that this was the case. While I accept that we cannot expect to accomplish much on the basis of our current observations, to deny the existence of a centre seems absurd.

I do not see how we can discover the structure of the universe without a fixed reference point. And, in my view, the centre is the only viable reference point.

Esteemed cosmologists, let us try the method that worked for Copernicus. Let us mentally position ourselves outside the universe. And let us bear in mind that densely compacted matter that has exploded tends to revolve around a centre. This is true of a star and its planets, and it is also true of a galactic system. Why would it not be true of the cosmos as a whole?

I would urge astronomers in all countries to adopt this hypothesis as a starting point for coordinated observations

– observations that might eventually result in the discovery of a structure. I, for one, would not be at all surprised to learn that the cosmos is a round made up of billions of star systems revolving around a centre.

Gentlemen of physics, you remain loyal to Einstein because the word of an emperor is law. But your loyalty does absolutely nothing to advance science.

It is time to jettison the manic tendency to reify artificial mathematical creations. For nature does not consist of reified mathematical formulas.

Nature consists of nature.

The little boy and the astronomer

Tell me, little boy, where do you live?
I live in Copernicus Street.
Where's that?
In The Hague.
Where's that?
In the Netherlands.
Where is that on the planet?
I don't know.

Tell me Professor, where do we humans live?
We live on planet Earth.
Where's that?
In the solar system.
Where's that?
In a galactic system.
Where is that in the universe?
I don't know.

22

A FINAL TRIBUTE TO MODERN SCIENCE

Dear Contemporaries,

Modern science began in the 16th century and, since then, it has made an important contribution to the development of knowledge and expertise. This process has advanced considerably and continues to accelerate, particularly when it comes to technology. Yet despite the rapid strides in our knowledge, we would have to admit that we have not made similar progress in understanding reality. In fact, there is a yawning chasm between the growth of knowledge and the generation of theories.

I have explained how the thinking that seeks to ascertain reality, which is practiced by modern scientists as assiduously as it has been practiced by priests, prophets and sages of all time, leads to the reification of conceptual notions and formulas, the mistaking of images for reality, and the failure to perceive the dynamics of evolution. As we have seen, ascertainment has resulted in an absurd worldview.

In other words, in failing to renew an obsolete way of thinking, modern science has failed to create a dynamic worldview and to develop a concept of man consistent with this new worldview. These things are of vital importance. It is essential that we identify principles that will guide both a renewal of our thinking and a renewal of the basis of our culture.

The modern era was a stage in the evolution of human culture. An important stage, yes, but a stage nonetheless: a link in a long chain of growing awareness. The wisdom developed by modern scientists will not stand the test of time – this is the fate of all wisdom. We have now reached the point where it is time for us to pay our final respects to modern thinking.

Modern science has failed to examine the phenomenon of evolution with a sufficiently open mind. Thinking that seeks to ascertain reality is inadequate to the task of describing a dynamically evolving reality. Hence scientific philosophy is undergoing a crisis. And this crisis is just one of the symptoms of a general cultural crisis.

Humankind is on the brink of a fundamental shift in human culture. Modern science is blind to the advance of a critical threshold. But then modern science was hampered by impaired vision from the start.

You, the representatives of modern science, have been blind to the fact that our current culture is still primitive. Your blindness to the reality of the situation is primarily due to your failure to view human culture from an evolutionary perspective.

But your blindness to the humanisation process that humankind is engaged in is even worse. In the latter days of your existence you have allowed the world to become less humane. Worse still is the fact that you have actively contributed to the decline of humanity by presenting your primitive contemporaries with tools that enable them to commit atrocities on a massive scale.

Farewell, modern science, you have had your day. You have played a positive role for several centuries, but you have now become an obstacle to the further advancement of human culture.

Farewell and rest in peace!

23

The essential factor that heralds renewal: a different attitude

Dear Contemporaries,

I can imagine that you may be irritated by the fact that I dismiss our current thinking as primitive. You may feel that you are being brushed aside like a small child. Or, worse still, like a primitive creature that has yet to shake off the vestiges of animalism.

But this is to misunderstand my argument. You are not primitive, our culture is primitive. Our thinking is essentially still in its infancy. This is a more realistic perspective than the one offered by some modern scientists, who would have us believe that we have now mapped and fathomed the depths of virtually all aspects of reality. All that is missing is a single mathematical formula, or so we are told.

Do you know what I think? I think modern scientists do not view things from a sufficient distance. So they lack the ability to view their own era and culture – and also their own efforts – with a critical eye.

I can offer scientists some good advice. You need to remove the spectacles that only allow you to see an ascertained reality. But, unfortunately, we are unlikely to find opticians who stock spectacles that enable scientists to see the world differently from the way they have seen it for the last ten thousand years.

Fortunately, as a scientist you have cultivated the ability to think for yourself. And if you want to perceive reality in a different way, you can. How? By adopting a critical stance in relation to the traditional way of thinking and the traditional notions that are considered to be scientifically valid. As an educated individual, you are capable of adopting an attitude towards existing concepts and theories that differs from the customary perspective.

Yes, I appreciate the fact that one of the most powerful lessons imparted to you by your education was that only those who have specialised to a considerable extent and made a name for themselves by publishing specialist articles, and who are then quoted as an authority on this basis, are regarded as proper scholars.

You may find it hard to imagine that individuals who have not done any research but who reflect on our existing culture and existing science can also make a contribution to science.

Yes, I know. Individuals such as these are not taken seriously by modern science. And you may be inclined to consider this the domain of philosophers, who these days are referred to as postmodernists. However, I have to say that, so far, I have been singularly unimpressed by the postmodernist critique of modern science.

"Hmmm," I think to myself. "All of these people supposedly received a good education."

"Mr Steenis," I hear you say, "All you have offered us is a negative critique. Where is the new thinking that you consider to be so essential?"

Well, since you ask... I still have a few more letters to write. I still have a few more ideas up my sleeve.

Potentiation - a fundamental feature of universal evolution

24

Evolution as a process of increasing complexity

Dear Contemporaries,

The world around us does not remain the same. It changes over time. Some three centuries ago people started to question whether it was possible to discern patterns in the changes that occurred over time.

Physicists ascertained that there always had been progressive development or 'evolution'. The earth started out as a molten mass. Over millions of years the outer surface of the molten mass cooled and solidified to form a crust. Geologists found evidence of evolution within the earth's crust and biologists discovered that there has been an enormous proliferation in the numbers of different species in the biosphere from the outset.

Those who familiarise themselves with the current body of knowledge in the realm of the natural sciences discover that the phenomenon of evolution exists in every domain of nature. Evolution manifests throughout the cosmos. So, while many scientists might still find it difficult to stomach the idea of cosmic evolution, there is no getting away from it: the universe, which encompasses the whole of reality, is characterised by evolution.

Physicists accepted the idea of evolution, albeit with some hesitation. Their hesitation was understandable. Newton, the founder of the philosophy on which modern science is based, asserted the existence of a fixed and unchanging worldview. The theory of evolution undermined this fundamental assumption. Modern scientists could not deny the principle of evolution: the facts confirm that evolution occurs. What could they do to reconcile the Newtonian worldview with the evidence provided by Darwin?

"We accept the reality of evolution," they said, "because

we do not consider that it involves essential change."

To me this seems to be a strange way of seeing things. Isn't there an essential difference between inert matter and living organisms? Isn't there an essential difference between a human being and an earthworm? Or at least between a human being and a mechanical device – even a device such as a computer? The natural scientists are resolute. The answer is no, absolutely not.

Yet why the emotional reaction? Why are scientists so reluctant to admit that evolution involves essential change? That we live in a world of constant change? The truth that scientists are unwilling to admit is that Newton got it wrong.

This is clearly a conundrum for modern science! But scientists are not that easily defeated. Their stock response is, "Yes, we agree that evolution produces change. But it does not introduce fundamental change. It only produces quantitative and measurable changes. Yes, over time nature creates new forms that are more complex than the ones they replace, but the fact that they are more complex does not mean that they are of an essentially different order.

In other words, the modern scientific view of evolution is that, in nature, the process of evolution simply introduces increasing complexity. Modern scientists cling to the idea of the homogeneity of nature, the principle of the 'uniformity of nature'.

I call this approach to reality 'all-the-same-ism'.

25

THE IDEA OF PROGRESS

Dear Contemporaries,

The idea of evolution was originally associated with the idea of progress. People believed that over the centuries human culture gradually evolved. This idea was one of the hallmarks of the Enlightenment in 18th-century Europe. The Enlightenment was an age of optimism. And the spirit of optimism flourished even more strongly in the 19th century. The belief in progress - a belief that growth would bring increasing prosperity and affluence - was embraced most strongly in England. People saw the economy and even all aspects of culture as being characterized by a process of steady upward growth.

However, German philosophers developed more nuanced ideas about progress. Rather than regarding progress as steady and continual development, they were more inclined to see it as a dialectic process. In other words, development was essentially a response to the collision of opposites. It arose out of the clash between the existing and the new. They accepted that, from time to time, during the course of its development, culture, for example, would undergo a period of crisis. This would mean that, on the one hand, culture would slide into a period of deep decline, yet at the same time renewal would begin to break new ground. Renewal would ultimately prevail, but only after a period of conflict and confusion.

The idea of progress itself played a significant role in the evolution of culture.

I imagine that the cultural scientists of the future will divide the development of philosophy into two periods: before and after the dawning of the idea of progress some three centuries ago.

In my view, people have yet to fully appreciate that this idea represented a fundamental change in human thinking.

The birth of this idea raised the barrier that stood in the way of deeper understanding.

A world of progress is a world that is constantly changing and the process of change is an agent of renewal. The old disappears to make way for the new. People do not always find it easy to accept this, because it introduces an element of uncertainty. For ten thousand years humans have shied away from uncertainty. To this day we want to be able to live with the reassurance of certainty - yet certainty is only afforded by the inevitable approach of death.

A world that is constantly changing poses additional problems for scientists. A world that is always in the process of renewing itself cannot be ascertained. The world-view that people have lived by for centuries is starting to crumble.

The idea that human culture evolves arose out of the understanding that culture becomes more sophisticated over time. Having arrived at this understanding, for the first time in history people welcomed change. The idea of progress began to spread. This was possible in a society in which culture was clearly flourishing.

In my view the birth of the idea of progress is the greatest mental revolution of all time. In the meantime the idea of progress has since celebrated its third millennium. But I don't see any bunting. As far as I can see, these days the idea of progress is as dead as a doornail.

This is because progress started out as a theory, but gradually changed into a belief. We don't have to do anything to create progress, it will happen all by itself. But of course that only applies if we don't put obstacles in the way of progress. Progress needs to have free rein. Culture needs to be given the kind of free rein that that allows nature to tolerate perpetual battle and competition.

The idea of progress has alternated between being present and absent. The belief in progress has waxed and waned in response to the ups and downs in the culture, and, more especially, the ups and downs in the economy. During and after the Second World War the belief in progress appeared to have been definitively extinguished, or so it seemed.

26

Evolution as a process of potentiation

Dear Contemporaries,

As I mentioned in my first letter, one of the faculty members who taught me during my time as a history student was Jan Romein. He was really more of a philosopher than a historian and he expounded his philosophical ideas in essays on the theory of history. In his essays he argued in favour of a dialectical interpretation of the human past. He was convinced we are currently experiencing a profound cultural crisis characterised by the collision of opposites. But, he said, such a crisis is the essential prerequisite for progress.

His colleagues had long since stopped believing in progress. Who would venture to speak of progress in the face of such unprecedented atrocities and violence? For the Second World War had barely ended when Romein began to express ideas that his peers thought were utter nonsense.

Nevertheless, Romein drew attention to the idea of dialectical development. In one of his essays on progress he pointed to the inherent contradiction of all progress. 'There is not one invention,' he wrote, 'that has not brought about both destruction and renewal. Let us liberate the concept of progress from value judgements. Advancement is inherent in historical development. Progress exists as an objective reality.'

In essence, he said, progress is a process in which, through the invention of culture, humans continually increase their ability to exploit more of the possibilities inherent in nature and, in doing so, they keep raising the level of culture. In other words, humans develop a growing range of new capabilities and these capabilities enable them to make what was previously impossible possible. This is something humans are able to do increasingly rapidly, especially in the areas of science and technology. Possibilities and capabilities can be collectively referred to as 'potencies'. Throughout the course of history we see the manifestation of a 'law of increasing potentiation'.

Jan Romein was seeking to identify the laws of history. "I practice theoretical history," he said. Looking back on what Romein wrote, I believe that there was something that he and his contemporaries failed to notice. They did not realise that he had turned away from the study of history and begun to venture into a new discipline. I call this new discipline the science of culture. I called for the recognition of this new discipline in my first letter, which discussed the importance of viewing things from a distance.

As I have already said, a scientific study of culture offers a perspective on the human past that is very different from the perspective offered by history. To this I would now add the following observation: since the dawn of culture, human advancement has been all about the development of potencies.

The practice of viewing things from a distance always leads the observer to think in terms of evolution. Without realising it, in seeking to identify the laws of history, Romein began to treat culture as an evolutionary process. Had he understood this and pursued this line of reasoning to its logical conclusion he would have acknowledged that the different epochs distinguished during the course of history are actually stages of development.

Romein called for the events of history to be viewed from a greater distance. This makes it possible to discern a dialectic pattern of evolution: a pattern in which each stage of development ends in a crisis, which is followed by the emergence of a new and more advanced stage. Each new stage is more advanced because it involves the discovery and development of new potentials.

Viewed from this perspective, the evolution of culture is a process of potentiation. But human culture is not the only aspect of reality that evolves. In the second half of the 20th century scientists discovered that the whole of reality evolves. Evolution is a universal phenomenon. On hearing this, my immediate response was to question whether the pattern that can be seen in the evolution of culture is any different from the pattern of evolution in general. Isn't the whole of reality characterised by a process of potentiation?

I am not a physicist, but to me it seems obvious that cosmic evolution is nothing more and nothing less than the continual emergence of new potencies. Molecules possess more potencies than atoms, chemical compounds possess more potencies than molecules, living cells possess more potencies than dead matter, plants and animals possess more potencies than cells, and humans possess more potencies than animals.

At every level evolution is a process that undergoes crises, which are essentially periods of stagnation. But, sooner or later, the process of emergence resumes as evolution creates the potencies that make it possible.

Evolution is a creative process – a process of essential qualitative renewal. And, by its very nature, it is both unascertainable and unpredictable.

Evolution is a universal phenomenon. The pattern of evolution is universal. The pattern amounts to potentiation.

Potentiation is the fundamental law of reality.

A new worldview

27

Contours of a new worldview

Dear Contemporaries,

A view of the cosmos that embraces the idea of potentiation sees a world of progressive stages that are essentially and qualitatively different. These stages often differ in terms of their complexity, but only their qualitative differences are fundamentally distinct.

Once again, this is not the view usually adopted in modern physics. Since the origins of modern science in the 17th century, its exponents have based their arguments on studies of reality that only recognise quantitative differences. Why? Because qualities are not measurable and they cannot be formulated in mathematical terms. So what do we do with qualities? We convert them to quantities!

Galileo put it like this: 'The great book of Nature lies ever open before our eyes... But we cannot read it unless we have first learned the language and the characters in which it is written... It is written in mathematical language. Natural phenomena are quantitative and therefore measurable. Where this does not appear to be the case, scientists have to conduct their experiments in such a way that the phenomena that are the subject of their experiments are rendered measurable.'

All scientists consider the principle of the 'uniformity of nature' to be an absolute and irrefutable certainty. The universe is a unified whole and everything within it must obey the same laws. This is the fundamental axiom of modern science and no dissent will be tolerated.

"Steenis is wasting his time if he imagines that this axiom will ever be discarded," I hear you say. "All modern thinkers, from Descartes to Einstein, have based their theories on the assumption that this principle is a certainty."

But what does Steenis say? I say, "The worldview that affirms the uniformity of nature has had its day! Nothing applies forever! Everything is evolving. Including our thinking! It is time to jettison the static thinking that seeks to ascertain reality and the fixed and static worldview that it engenders.

It is generally known that life on earth evolved from simple and primitive beginnings. But these primitive evolutionary origins eventually led to the emergence of human beings. Less widely known, and less accepted, is the fact that the inorganic matter that exists today can also be traced back to very primitive forms, but during the course of almost fourteen billion years the evolution of inorganic matter has led to the diversity we now see in the universe.

I say the universe is the product of stages of evolution and that these stages of evolution all introduce qualitative differences. Far from there being 'uniformity', there is tremendous diversity in reality. The universe is a continuous progression of stages, all of which possess their own qualities and these qualities are characterised by their own processes, structures and laws.

Each new stage emerges out of a crisis. From time to time development stagnates. The next new stage can only emerge once new potencies, which did not previously exist, have been created. The evolution of matter, life and culture is a process of potentiation. Far from being 'uniform', the cosmos consists of spheres of potency that are essentially different.

28

A PROBLEM THAT CANNOT BE SOLVED BY MODERN SCIENCE

Dear Contemporaries,

I speak of a metabletic approach to reality. The term derives from a Greek verb that means 'to undergo change' or 'to become changed'. The approach is based on a philosophy that proceeds from the assumption that we live in a changing, evolving reality, an evolving universe. The starting point of this philosophy can be summarised very simply as: evolution is universal.

If you read my previous letters, you may have needed to catch your breath as you realised the implications. The world as you knew it (a reified worldview, to be more precise) collapsed. I imagine that, at this point, your first question is, "If what you say is right, how am I supposed to come to terms with the reality of a world that is always changing, a reality that is devoid of any certainty?"

Yes. It is difficult to make the transition from an old philosophy to a new philosophy. This was also the case in the past. And I will be the first to admit that the transition I am calling for is very radical. What I am calling for is nothing less than a new way of thinking, a new approach to everything that exists. But if you read on you will discover that the metabletic approach provides a context in which fundamental problems are resolved.

Today's physicists are struggling with what they see as a basic problem. The physics of subatomic particles is not theoretically consistent with the physics of other physical phenomena. They have yet to develop a theory that would unite and explain all physical phenomena. They have tried to find a solution by formulating theories based on mathematical reasoning that propose the existence of many dimensions. But their efforts have been in vain.

Yet is there really a problem? If we adopt the metabletic view, the answer is no. For the sake of argument, let us agree that reality manifests as a series of stages that exhibit increasing potencies. The earliest stage will exhibit less comprehensive potencies than the stages that follow. All beginnings are primitive, and this also applies to the beginnings of cosmic evolution. Given that this is the case, the quest to develop a 'theory of everything' is unrealistic, for, in principle, it is impossible to construct a theory that explains everything – or at least this certainly holds true in a universe that is thought to be 'uniform'.

The solution? Abandon the principle of the 'uniformity of nature' and accept the premise that there are spheres of potency, stages of evolution that are essentially and qualitatively different. The physicists of the future will be faced with the task of identifying the fundamental stages of evolution in the unfolding of the cosmos, and the levels of development within each stage. Yet the criterion that will enable a systematic analysis of an evolving reality will always be the growth in potency.

In other words, what we find is that the problem of the missing 'theory of everything' is actually only an apparent problem. It forms part of a worldview produced by thinking that seeks to ascertain reality. This way of thinking is bewildered by the phenomenon of evolution and equally bewildered by the idea of an evolving universe.

The reality that exists at a subatomic level is a stage of lesser potency. As such, it cannot be encompassed by a formula that explains stages that exhibit more advanced potencies.

It is fundamentally impossible to construct a 'theory of everything' if the universe is thought to be uniform.

29

ANOTHER PROBLEM THAT CANNOT BE SOLVED: THE QUESTION OF MAN´S PLACE IN THE UNIVERSE

Dear Contemporaries,

Over the centuries people have sought to explain man's place in relation to the surrounding reality. And modern scientists continue to grapple with the question of what view of man is consistent with our view of reality? But no one has yet come up with a satisfactory answer.

How would we approach this from a metabletic point of view?

Firstly we would see man as a product of the evolution of the universe – a being of cosmic origins. During the course of cosmic evolution, early forms of matter progressed through a series of stages that exhibited increasingly advanced potencies. In other words, the potencies that emerge at each successive stage of evolution introduce more advanced capabilities than the potencies that went before.

In terms of cosmic evolution, human beings are a very recent phenomenon. Hence the metabletic view would suggest that human potencies must be highly advanced. Is this the case?

To answer this question we would need to study human potencies in great detail. But psychology as it exists today does not adopt this approach. The human mind is seen as a set of functions rather than a repository of potencies. And since a systematic study of human potencies has yet to be conducted, at the moment there is little that can be said. However, in the meantime we can formulate hypotheses based on personal impressions and experiences.

This is what I have done. In other words, the question I have sought to answer is: how advanced are the potencies possessed by human beings, when considered from the metabletic perspective?

This question poses a particularly complicated problem. Why? Because the potency that characterises human beings above all others is unique. That potency is the human mind.

And this brings us to an issue that has preoccupied philosophers and scientists for centuries: namely, what is the place of the human mind within the whole of reality? Or, to put it another way, what is the relationship between the material and the immaterial, between matter and mind, between the concrete and the abstract?

This is a well-known issue in philosophy and science. It is usually referred to as the brain-mind problem.

It is the most controversial issue addressed by human beings and it has never been resolved. In my view, it cannot be resolved within the conceptual framework of modern science.

But the metabletic view provides an answer – an answer reminiscent of Columbus and the egg!

30

The solution of the brain-mind problem

Dear Contemporaries,

Where does the world of mental phenomena fit within the universe? How do we resolve the duality between matter and mind?

There is a confusing array of answers to this question. The only thing they have in common is that none of them are widely accepted. Mental activity, such as thinking, is more than simply the activity of the brain. Yet the mind cannot be separated from the brain. Given this apparent paradox, how can the relationship between the mind and the brain be scientifically explained?

The latest line of reasoning to be added to the array of answers is that thinking exists, but it is the brain that thinks: the body is the passive agent of the brain.

So now you know! It is your brain that determines what you think and feel and what you do or don't do. Unsurprisingly, many modern scientists consider this theory to be unacceptable. They recognise that the human mind is an independent entity. But how do they perceive the relationship between the mind and the brain?

The fact is, they don't really have an answer. Philosophers have been pondering this for centuries, but they have failed to find a satisfactory solution. Is the problem beyond the capability of the human mind? Not necessarily, but it cannot be solved by those who embrace an 'it's all the same' worldview, which assumes that the universe is essentially uniform. Of course the brain and the mind do not form part of a homogeneous uniform whole. They are two vastly different things! The mind cannot be reduced to the activity of neurons, synapses, electrochemical signals and other material interactions. The mind is of a different, higher order.

The problem can be solved if we accept that the world is constantly evolving and that the process of evolution introduces new and more advanced potencies. There are spheres of increasing potency that range from primitive states of matter to more complex organisations of matter. There is a subatomic sphere, a chemosphere and a biosphere. The mental phenomena do not fit within any of these spheres. Given that this is the case, I say we need to recognise the existence of another sphere of potency: the psychosphere!

In other words, the solution of the brain-mind problem can be summarized as follows: the material brain and the immaterial mind originate from different spheres of potency. The material and the immaterial cannot be grouped in the same category. Again the problem is only an apparent problem.

In short, the mind does not occupy space, it does not have any mass and it does not emit radiation. In terms of the variables commonly used in physics, the mind does not exist. And yet it is clearly a phenomenon that exists within the cosmos. The mental dimension of existence harbours immense potencies, more advanced potencies than all of the preceding spheres of potency. The psychosphere is the most recent and least understood sphere of potency that we are aware of.

A hypothesis that sees the psychosphere as a sphere of potency that forms part of reality puts an end to the duality between matter and mind. It also puts an end to the divide between the natural sciences and the humanities.

Yet at the same time it raises another question: what gave rise to the emergence of such a unique sphere of potency that is so different from the other spheres?

The answer to this question will have to be formulated as a series of hypotheses.

I discuss these hypotheses in the letters that follow.

A NEW VIEW OF MAN

31

What gave rise to the phenomenon of the mind?

Dear Contemporaries,

The phenomenon of the mind must have evolved out of the sphere of potency that emerged immediately prior to the psychosphere. In other words, the earliest mental processes must have arisen out of the biosphere. But the biosphere itself evolved through innumerable intermediate stages. Mental processes certainly did not spring from the most primitive forms of life that existed billions of years ago. They must have emanated from more evolved forms of life.

I suspect that at a certain point in biotic evolution the first single-celled organisms appeared on earth. The formation of a cell represented a significant increase in potency, yet it also had a drawback in that the cell wall separated the organism from its environment to a greater or lesser extent. But since an organism has to obtain food from its environment, contact with the environment is vital in enabling an organism to survive and procreate.

I also suspect that, to compensate for the loss of physical contact with the environment, single-celled organisms developed a new potency that enabled them to mentally become one with their environment. The cell wall developed the ability to 'sense' the environment through becoming one with it. The organisms were then no longer entirely dependent on chance when it came to finding food. From that point on the cell wall operated as the precursor of the senses. I call the ability to mentally become one with the environment 'empathic capacity'.

The emergence of multicellular organisms made it possible for certain cells to concentrate on particular functions. This enabled multicellular organisms to develop rudimentary senses. And, since these early forms of life were only able to survive in a watery environment, the first senses to evolve would have been the contact senses of taste and touch. The development and use of these senses would have considerably increased the organisms' empathic capacity.

The operation of the senses requires the presence of a primitive nervous system – a kind of relay centre that receives stimuli and transmits corresponding signals to a motor system. When stimuli are relayed into action there can be said to be a stimulus-response process.

However, the response is a direct and automatic response that is always the same. The organism does not have the ability to reflect and is not consciously aware of its environment. I believe this to be the origin of the realms of famous unconscious, which include the human unconscious.

The next thing we need to consider is whether there was any inner experience of sensation at this early stage. There is little we can say about this. But at a certain point empathic forms of life began to register sensations of hunger and satiation, pain and pleasure, heat and cold.

With the registering of these sensations we arrive at the phenomenon of inner experience, the phenomenon of sensate awareness.

The earliest mental processes must be seen as empathic capacities. At this point they are still relatively limited potencies.

But evolution always continues. And eventually new mental potencies emerge.

32

How did the mind evolve?

Dear Contemporaries,

Every so often evolution can be seen to stagnate, but sooner or later there is a breakthrough and progress resumes.

This was no different in the psychosphere. Evolution did not stop at the contact senses. The need to compete for resources may have contributed to the emergence of new distance senses. The newly evolved organisms equipped with distance senses could smell, see and hear. In other words, these organisms were equipped with more advanced potencies.

Organisms that only received input through empathic senses could only sense their environment, whereas the newly evolved forms of life could not only sense their environment but also perceive food and danger. Empathic sensing triggers a response to stimuli but the environment remains meaningless. The process of perception starts to result in the development of a more detailed picture of the surrounding world. The nervous system continued to evolve – it had to. Organisms equipped with distance senses had to be able to interpret a profusion of impressions: What is this? And what does it mean? The organisms started to become aware of the world around them. In other words, they began to form a very primitive worldview.

It was this process that gave rise to consciousness. To survive organisms have to gather knowledge of the world around them and store it so they can retrieve it. This results in the development of memory. The storage and retrieval of knowledge requires new and far more advanced brain functioning. This is essentially a new approach to the world, a new stage within the evolution of the psychosphere.

Conscious thought and deliberate action are the product of a new potency. This is actually a whole new capacity that I call 'epistemic capacity'. There is a fundamental difference between empathy and epistemic ability: it is essentially the difference between unconscious existence and conscious existence.

So can animate nature be divided into empathic and epistemic organisms? Apparently not. Organisms that possess epistemic ability do not lose their empathic capacity. In the evolution of the psychosphere both capacities are retained.

And evolution did not end there. There was a third step in the evolution of the mind. The nervous system of relatively recently evolved organisms, by which I mean higher mammals and humans, developed to the point where empathy and epistemic ability are able to work together. I call this third mental potency the 'noetic capacity'.

My view is based on the assumption that these three capacities – empathy, epistemic ability and the noetic faculty – are more highly developed in humans than in any other animal.

Does our experience as human beings confirm this assumption? I believe so. I invite you to join me in examining your personal experience in this light.

33

The metabletic view of the unconscious

Dear Contemporaries,

In the current scientific paradigm psychology is a science of cognitive mental processes. Cognition is a concept derived from the study of information and communication. Both disciplines owe their existence to the development of the computer. In other words, cognitive psychology is a field in which language and other symbols play a primary role.

Whichever way you look at it, it is difficult to escape the fact that if psychological activity is considered to be similar to the workings of a computer, psychology as a discipline will inevitably confine itself to the study of conscious mental processes, such as perception, conceptualisation, the storage of memories, interpretation, analysis, problem solving and learning. In the previous letter I suggested that, from the metabletic point of view, all of these processes are considered to fall in just one of the mental capacities possessed by humans, namely human epistemic capacity.

This approach is clearly inspired by the main function of a computer, which is to process information. The invention and development of the computer is undoubtedly a technological achievement of the highest order. In fact, it is impossible to imagine modern culture without computers. Besides providing access to an inexhaustible source of knowledge, computers also create connections between people of all continents. The speed with which computers can solve mathematical problems and perform other tasks is unrivalled. Computers are even said to possess intelligence – that is to say artificial intelligence. But then a definition of intelligence is omitted.

Seen from a metabletic point of view, cognitive psychology simply studies human epistemic capacity. But that is only one of the capacities possessed by human beings. Our empathic capacity is also very highly developed. Cognitive psychology's failure to acknowledge and address this capacity can be explained by the fact that it involves unconscious mental activity – and there is no such equivalent in a computer.

In my view, other fields of psychology have also failed to advance our understanding of unconscious processes. Modern thinking does not concern itself with these forms of mental activity. If there is a single phenomenon that modern science has singularly failed to explain, it is the human psyche, the conscious and unconscious functions of the human mind.

While modern scientists repudiate introspection, I believe it is in our interest for us to develop greater awareness of our empathic responses. This means we have to make an effort to become conscious of unconscious processes. Few people do this nowadays. Freud originally tried to shed light on the subject, but, in my view, his initial assumptions were not a valid starting point.

Empathic capacity is old in evolutionary terms. At one stage it was the only form of mental processing that existed and it too evolved over time. Psychobiologists might wish to take up the worthy challenge of studying and identifying the developmental stages of human empathic capacity, for this is an area that has yet to be comprehensively studied.

In the meantime let us consider how we experience our own empathic capacity.

Human beings clearly possess highly developed empathic abilities. This is confirmed by thousands of personal experiences that I and others can point to. Let me start by talking about my own experience. I am sure that as I mention a few examples of empathic responses you will be able to relate them to your own experience.

Empathic responses encompass such a wide range of internal phenomena that it is difficult to know where to begin, but let me list a few categories.

Unconscious merging, sensing, involuntary actions, impulses, unconscious enjoyment of colours, sounds and social atmospheres, shared enthusiasm, being overwhelmed by a landscape, the ocean, a crowd, a starry sky, a demonstration, a state of religious rapture, being swept up by the mentality of a group – even if it is antisocial or out of control, reactions triggered by emotional memories, performing a routine procedure without having to think about it, being overcome by jealousy, envy, horror or awe. In other words, empathic responses include all of the things we do unconsciously, things we do without a second thought, and reactions triggered by moods and impulses.

You will agree that it is a long list. Empathic responses, attuning to and merging with our environment, and emotional and unconscious reactions form a large part of our existence and experience.

When we respond empathically to the world around us we literally make our environment come alive. We actually transfer some of our own aliveness to the people and things we resonate with. We walk through a park and see weeping willows draped over a pond. Do willows actually weep? No, of course not! But something about their drooping branches reminds us of how we feel when we shed tears. We experience a similar kind of empathic merging when we swim in the sea. After a while we feel that we are becoming one with the ocean. And if you lie outside on a lawn or in a field on a summer night and look up at the stars, after a while you will start to experience something that makes you feel dizzy. You will feel as if you are a particle floating through the cosmos. It is also possible to feel that you are one with nature and an integral part of creation. This is essentially an experience of mystical union.

You may also find yourself being enraptured by a piece

of music. You don't need to know anything about the music to be enchanted by the sounds. The same kind of thing can happen when you look at a beautiful painting. You feel deeply moved without being able to explain why.

And, as you may know from your own experience, it is not uncommon for the sound of running water to trigger the urge to urinate.

A similar overwhelming sense of union is experienced in a football stadium. The supporters are one with the team they revere so highly. When one of their heroes scores, they rise en mass, cheer and sing and dance about. Sometimes they even physically attack those who support the opposing team or those who are there to maintain order in the stadium. The player who scored the goal races to the side of the stadium where his supporters are gathered. He and the supporters both cling to the railings between them because they feel a powerful need to connect with each other physically. Why all the emotion? The answer is obvious. As far as the supporters are concerned, they are the heroes who scored!

And while we are on the subject, the need to connect with each other physically deserves a chapter all of its own. We hug and kiss. We cuddle up next to each other and stroke each other. We also stroke our pets – and they love it. Why do we have such a strong bond with our dog or cat? Why does a housewife develop such a close bond with her parrot? The same thing occurs between a dolphin trainer and the dolphins they train and between a rider and their horse. And that's without mentioning the bond between lovers.

How is it that we are able to train a dog to be a guide dog? And how does a rider get their horse to execute complex dressage movements and soar over jumps? This cannot be achieved by showing the animal a textbook. Needless to say, there has to be a profound connection between human and animal!

Television soap operas are tremendously popular. What causes viewers to get so emotionally caught up in the lives of the characters? It is their empathic identification with the characters. They feel that what is happening to the characters is happening to them – even if they are not conscious of it.

Those who produce television commercials know this from their own experience. They don't need to be convinced by theoretical analysis. Their commercials usually feature characters experiencing a strong emotion – in most cases delirious joy. This kind of advertising started with a detergent commercial. Two next-door neighbours are out in the garden hanging washing on the line. One of the women suddenly looks totally crestfallen. "Your laundry is so much whiter than mine!" she says to her neighbour. Whereupon her neighbour triumphantly informs her, "That's because I use detergent X!" These kinds of commercials rely entirely on the viewer's unconscious empathic identification with the characters in the commercial.

If you ask an impersonator which vocal muscles he uses and how he alters his pronunciation and the tone of his voice, he will be unable to tell you. The answer is, he makes all of the necessary adjustments by unconsciously resonating with the character he is impersonating.

Schools teach foreign languages by making children learn rules of grammar and syntax and memorise lists of vocabulary. We are convinced that knowledge has to be acquired through the use of our epistemic abilities. But send a pupil to a country where the language is spoken and arrange for them to stay with a family that cannot speak any other language for six or seven weeks and on their return they will be speaking the language fluently! Needless to say, this is also how a baby learns to speak its native language!

The way mothers and baby play together is a model example of empathic union. The mother never has to explain what the game is, or the rules of the game, but the baby naturally engages in the game and gurgles with delight! Similarly, we don't have to teach our dog how to play. Dogs and children automatically know how to play and both derive great pleasure from it!

So far we have been looking at examples of unconscious empathic union. Now I would like to examine how unconscious impressions resurface, sometimes years later.

Our empathic capacities are older than our epistemic abilities in evolutionary terms. As individual organisms we also go through a stage of empathic development before we discover our epistemic abilities. As babies we hear language around us but we ourselves can't speak, read, write or count. We don't know how to interpret our surroundings or what is happening around us, but we sense and respond to our surroundings and what happens to us. Of course we don't remember any of this later because empathic sensing is an unconscious process and the associated memories are also unconscious.

Yet the memory of an incident that was experienced entirely at an empathic level can surface again later. To give you an example, let's say a young mother is walking down the street holding her little boy's hand. Suddenly the two are faced with a large dog on a leash. The dog barks loudly and bares its teeth. It leaps towards them and almost tears loose. What does the mother do? She immediately picks up her toddler and runs away from the dog, while telling the child not to be afraid. The little boy screams and cries and struggles violently. Despite his mother's reassurance he is frightened by the incident. The sight of the dog's flashing teeth, the loud bark, the hasty departure from the scene – everything merges into a single experience of terror that is stored in his empathic memory as jumble of sensory impressions, overwhelming emotions and irrepressible urges that drive the motor system. I call this kind of memory, which always contains all three elements (sense impressions, emotions and motor impulses), an 'empathic attitude'. The recall of the memory may be triggered by a nightmare, or if the child encounters an intimidating dog in another situation. The empathic attitude will then immediately resurface and will instil the same fear and the same urge to run away. (The sensory impressions retained as a result of such an incident are usually the impressions seen and heard through the distance senses. In other words, this part of an empathic attitude is epistemic, which will facilitate the recall of the incident.)

An empathic attitude is often formed by a negative experience. And, as we all know, a severely distressing event can result in psychological trauma. But the impressions created by positive experiences are also retained as empathic attitudes. Allow me to share an example from my own life. When she was at home, my mother used to sing all kinds of songs. As a child I experienced the sound of her singing empathically. I couldn't understand the words, but I registered the sound of the melody and the lyrics. When I was older I heard the sounds again and experienced something remarkable. I recalled the sounds and, as I now understand it, relived my empathic response as a young boy. It was an extraordinary experience! This also explains the phenomenon of nostalgia.

Is it also possible for people to act empathically? Yes. You yourself will undoubtedly have experienced this. Empathic action in response to an unexpected situation can be immediate. This is what occurs if you are suddenly confronted with a rapidly approaching obstacle when driving on the motorway. In such a situation it is probably not advisable to take time to reflect on the best course of action! There is also such a thing as impulsive action. We do something just like that, without any deliberation. Some people might say we are being guided by our emotions. But it is important not to lose sight of the fact that any empathic impression always includes an emotional component. When we act empathically, our actions are dictated by an empathic attitude.

There is also such a thing as involuntary behaviour. Someone swears at you and you feel offended. In such a situation it is almost inevitable that your first impulse will be to respond with a similar insult. But if you are sensible you will suppress the urge to react impulsively. If you do this, your reaction is then a conscious reaction mediated by your epistemic faculties.

To give a very different example, if we are among a group of people who are convulsed with laughter, we have a tendency to laugh with them – even if we have absolutely no idea why they are laughing. Similarly, if we are with someone who keeps yawning, we often start yawning too. Gang mentality can be equally infectious. If a group of kids are out on the street and the more belligerent members of the group start kicking over rubbish bins, the others generally follow suit.

Empathic behaviour can be automatic. We unconsciously maintain our balance when we are walking, cycling and skating. And we perform a complex set of procedures without thinking about it when driving a car. We can even read automatically. If a teacher asks a twelve-year-old to read a passage aloud, the pupil may read the passage aloud perfectly. Yet if the teacher asks the pupil to comment on what is written in the text, they are likely to be met with a look of total bewilderment. For the pupil automatically converted the words on the page into spoken language without registering the content.

But let me summarise.

The role that our empathic capacities play in our lives should not be underestimated. Our emotions are inextricably associated with our empathic attitudes. As well as perceiving the world, at the same time we also sense the world. In other words, we register the world around us and this provokes deep feelings. Our lives would be unimaginably impoverished at a mental level if we did not possess such highly developed empathic capacities!

With some hesitation, I would like to end with a hypothesis. Could it be that an organism's empathic union with its tangible surroundings influenced its evolution? Could it be that empathy enabled organisms to successfully respond and adapt to their surroundings? In other words, could it be that evolution was not simply a matter of fortuitous mutations in the genome, but also determined by an organism's unconscious capacity to register and respond to its environment?

Whatever the case, let us start by conducting a thorough study of the phenomenon of empathy as I have defined it.

34

Human epistemic capacity

Dear Contemporaries,

It is through our epistemic capacity that we become aware of ourselves and the world around us.

There is a distinct difference between human empathic capacity and human epistemic capacity. Both serve the same purpose in enabling us to communicate with our surroundings. Yet our empathic faculties operate through the contact senses and rely on physical contact for information, while our epistemic faculties operate through the distance senses, so in this case distance plays a primary role. We sense something empathically through becoming one with our surroundings, yet our epistemic faculties require that we separate ourselves from our surroundings. These two mental capacities operate very differently and utilise different pathways within the nervous system.

As creatures endowed with epistemic abilities, human beings do what their distance senses enable them to do: they explore the world. This involves wanting to know. It also involves acquiring knowledge and storing it as a memory that can be recalled and used when needed.

If knowledge were stored in a completely random way, it would be impossible to retrieve it. To be able to find a particular book in your bookcase, for example, you need to arrange your books in a certain order. Similarly, in order to function effectively, we need to structure our knowledge. Otherwise it would be impossible for us to carry out tasks and make plans.

To structure our knowledge we have to be able to place newly acquired knowledge among all of our other epistemic experiences. Every experience has to be grasped. To grasp originally meant to grasp with the hands: we have to get a grip on things. We are continually converting impressions received through our distance senses into concepts and then ordering these concepts. Of course, the way we order concepts differs depending on our age, our environment and our own unique character.

I suspect that our empathic memories are arranged very differently. For in this case we are storing empathic attitudes, which are a jumble of sensory impressions, emotionally charged sense impressions and irrepressible urges that drive the motor system. These attitudes are ordered through the principle of association, which means that similar attitudes are grouped together. Hence attitudes tinged with sadness are stored together in our memory and one sad memory will often lead us to recall another.

But back to epistemic ability. The process of perception, comprehension, storage of knowledge and retrieval of memories includes forming associations between experiences, which is how we develop a worldview. This is essentially a concept of the world based on the sum total of our knowledge, which shapes our understanding of the world. Everything we learn on a daily basis contributes to the gradual formation of our worldview. This is how we grow into the culture that surrounds us. We learn to ascertain a world.

Humans live in communities. The functioning of our epistemic faculties involves continual communication with fellow human beings. Through empathic attunement we unconsciously form part of a community or group. Our epistemic faculties require the use of symbols, such as gestures, sounds, language and letters.

Innumerable volumes have been published on the subject of conscious behaviour, which encompasses a vast range of activities. I have little to add. All I would say is that I believe the inner workings of human experience generally rely on the combined functioning of our empathic and epistemic abilities, which is how I define human noetic capacity. The mental processes studied by cognitive psychologists are usually not simply epistemic activity (they refer to it as cognitive activity), but noetic activity.

35

Human noetic capacity

Dear Contemporaries,

In evolutionary terms the noetic faculty is the amalgamation of empathic and epistemic ability. Together these two capacities create a capacity of a higher order. The noetic faculty is the latest stage in the evolution of the psychosphere.

The noetic faculty emerged relatively recently. We take it for granted that we can sense and perceive at the same time, that we can act as swiftly as an arrow and think about what we are doing at the same time, that we can immerse ourselves in an environment and objectively assess our surroundings at the same time. Yet the development of this capacity distinguishes humans from the majority of life on earth. The noetic faculty is an exceptional capacity. Their highly advanced noetic capacity enabled humans to rise to the top of the psychosphere.

The different memory processes associated with our empathic and epistemic capacities are also able to operate simultaneously. In other words, empathic attitudes and epistemic concepts, and associations between concepts, can be recalled in relation to each other – with unprecedented results. Allow me to recount a personal experience that illustrates how this can work.

I was watching television on the first day of the last European football championship. Russia was playing against the Czech Republic. Russian spectators were waving their national flag, which consists of equal horizontal white, blue and red stripes. I proceeded to tell my fellow viewers an old anecdote about the origin of the Russian flag. The Russian word for 'flag' derives from the Dutch word for 'flag'.

During his visit to the Netherlands, Peter the Great was so struck by the beauty of the Dutch flag that he made a slight modification and adopted it as the Russian national flag.

That night I woke up with a melody playing through my mind. It was not the kind of music you hear every day. I tried to place it, and, after a while, I realised that it was the music of the clog dance in the Zar und Zimmermann opera composed by Albert Lortzing.

What I think must have happened is this: epistemic input (the discussion of the origin of the Russian flag) triggered my empathic memory, which had apparently registered and stored the music of Lortzing's clog dance. My noetic faculty was clearly at work during the night. Hence my nighttime recall of music associated with Tsar Peter the Great.

It is not uncommon for our empathic and epistemic memories to be at odds with each other in terms of their content. Empathic attitudes are largely born out of experiences that stem back to our childhood and are heavily coloured by the specific circumstances of our individual lives. Emotions always pay a significant role in empathic attitudes. When it comes to the content of epistemic memories, this is not the case. We accumulate most of the content of our epistemic memories during social interaction, primarily in the family, at school and beyond. The divide between these two sets of memories can be the cause of mental problems. People feel ashamed or confused. Yet this is unwarranted for the human psyche is inevitably full of contradictions.

The noetic faculty combines two layers of communication. Through communication we form a commune or community. Empathic communication is involuntary and occurs unconsciously. Epistemic communication is a conscious process. We have to actively establish and maintain epistemic communication. We have to gesture, wave, call, speak, sing, write... We detect the unconscious attitudes and unconscious behaviour of our fellow human beings through our empathic abilities. We ascertain their views and intentions through our epistemic faculties. Our noetic faculties enable us do both of these things simultaneously. These two layers of communication combine to form a noetic experience.

Our noetic faculties are the 'tool' we use to gain insight and develop understanding. They allow us to grasp connections that remain invisible when we rely entirely on our epistemic abilities. Our ability to see connections between facts turns isolated facts into a meaningful whole so we can then form a theory. Sometimes a dream will reveal a connection that our epistemic capacities fail to detect.

Insight and understanding can lead to self-reflection. This, in turn, contributes to the formation of the personality, which is essentially the sum total of the noetic attitudes held by an individual. Personality arises out of the interaction between an individual and their environment.

During the course of social interaction people confront each other as personalities. In other words, they confront each other with their noetic attitudes. Sometimes these are empathic attitudes formed during childhood that are then later defended with epistemic arguments in adulthood. Within the context of social relationships, a primitive empathic attitude, such as an instinctive dislike of those who are perceived as 'other' for example, is regarded as a 'prejudice'.

We see the same epistemisation in debates on ethics. Ethicists are always talking about standards and values. However, in my view, the actions of football fans who come to blows with the supporters of the opposing team are dictated by primitive empathic attitudes. Standards and values have nothing to do with it! I came across an extreme example of epistemisation when reading and essay by a professional in the field of cognitive psychology, who claimed that babies quickly start developing standards and values! Maybe the fact that babies now attend lectures on ethics has escaped my notice.

In public debate and political propaganda it is standard practice for people to couch primitive attitudes in loftier epistemic terms. The most shocking example of this, that I am aware of, is the way we, as a human community, treat the noetic attitudes of humanity and barbarity. We only prosecute those who behave inhumanely if they break a law. Our current societies do not aspire to instil an attitude of true humanity in their members. In other words, as long as we don't break a law, we are free to bully, torment and mentally abuse others as much as we like. War criminals are occasionally arrested, tried and convicted now that international courts can find that atrocities such as genocide, mass slaughter and torture are 'crimes against humanity'. Having said this, instances of war criminals being prosecuted are relatively rare. The powers that would make this possible and the means of exercising those powers have yet to be put in place in the current political world order.

Lastly, by definition, the noetic faculty endows us with creative ability. Without the noetic faculty there would be no imagination. And without imagination there would be no literature, no films, no television drama, no stage arts, no music and no visual arts. And through the process of intuition the noetic faculty also enables us to conceive new ideas, make discoveries and create inventions.

In other words, the noetic faculty is the source of all creativity and creative endeavour. Humans became the rulers of the earth thanks to their noetic capacity. The noetic faculty operates in a powerful brain with very advanced mental capacities. We may consider ourselves fortunate that we are gifted with such remarkable abilities.

Of course, we would also be well advised to make good use of these abilities!

The dawn of a new era

36

A STAGE OF CULTURAL EVOLUTION IS NEARING ITS END

Dear Contemporaries,

If it were possible for us to go back in time and ask one of the leading figures of the Renaissance, "Don't you think it's remarkable that you are witnessing the dawning of a new era in history," they would not have understood the question. In those days there was no concept of stages of history. The person you spoke to might have said, "Why do you speak of renewal? We are simply reviving something that already exists. Charlemagne revived the Roman Empire by becoming the Caesar of his day. And many have since followed in his footsteps. The ancient Greeks and Romans were the founders of civilization. There's nothing that can be done to improve civilization."

So why do we modern humans adopt a different perspective? How is it that we are able to identify different historical eras? It is because we are viewing the past from a greater distance. And when we view the past from a greater distance, we don't look at years, but at centuries or even millennia. This enables us to perceive the overall pattern of order that runs through the chaos of events. We can do this when we look at the past. The question is, can we also see our own era a stage that forms part of a much larger process of evolution?

I have my doubts. Although we are now clearly capable of viewing our own era as a stage in a much longer process of development, for us to perceive our era in this way, something else is required. We need to realise that the process of development is occurring over a much longer period than we would normally consider.

It is precisely because we are not used to thinking in terms of such long periods that my views come across as strange. My frame of reference differs from the conventional frame of reference. I base my thinking on my understanding of metabletics, and this requires that we view everything from a greater distance and entertain the possibility that developments occur over far longer time frames than we currently realise.

I came to the conclusion that, until recently, the human species, Homo sapiens, existed as an animal among animals, and that culture is therefore a relatively recent phenomenon. If this is indeed the case, it is hardly surprising that human inner nature and human behaviour still exhibit many animal traits. Humans who enter the world of culture gradually outgrow the vestiges of their animal past and their own animal tendencies. Cultural evolution involves many aspects, but the foremost aspect is the ascent from animal existence to human existence. Cultural evolution is a process of becoming truly human, a process of humanisation.

Like all forms of evolution, humanisation is a process that occurs over very long periods. It also happens in stages. It is not easy for humans to shake off their animal past. During the course of my life I have had the misfortune to witness the animal behaviour that people are capable of.

Historians often refer to human culture as it currently exists as 'civilization'. But, in my lexicon, the term civilization suggests a far more advanced culture. A culture characterised by true humanity. But then I suppose historians would also describe totalitarian regimes, such as those headed by Hitler and Stalin, as 'civilized'.

Am I denying the true state of affairs? Some would argue that the balance shifted from animal to human when human communities began to elect state governments, and that, from that point on, such communities can automatically be regarded as civilized. But in my younger years I saw nations that were thought of as highly civilized exercise unbridled bloodlust. The Second World War was a display of animal behaviour – and not only by the Nazis. And since the Second World War there have been acts of genocide in many places throughout the world, to say nothing of all of the other acts of brutality. It is ridiculous for our culture as it currently exists to be described as 'civilization'.

It is time for us to ask ourselves how far we, as modern individuals, have advanced along the road to true civilization and true humanity. Just how humane are we?

We consider it quite normal that some of us lead billionaire lifestyles while others starve to death. That society is dominated by a ruthless determination to amass wealth and power - a ruthless determination that increasingly resorts to corruption, fraud and crime to achieve its own ends and abandons any hint of humanity. We consider it quite normal that the superpowers rack up multi-billion dollar defence budgets in order to prepare for dreadful wars, ostensibly 'in the interest of freedom and justice'. It is not uncommon for hundreds of thousands of people to have to flee their homes in order to escape violence. Yet it seems this is simply the order of the day.

As far as I am concerned, the worst thing about all of this is that we have yet to formulate a plan to put an end to this mess – a plan to make the world humane. We prefer to turn a blind eye to the fact that our so-called 'civilization' is rife with barbarity.

But, after all, why should we bother to develop such a plan? Surely the mess that our world has become is normal?

37

Are we heading towards our downfall?

Dear Contemporaries,

For the last five centuries Europe has been the epitome of so-called 'civilization'. During the course of these five centuries, the period referred to as the modern era, Europeans gradually conquered the world. They gained ascendancy over the other inhabitants of the planet through their technological achievements and by developing science. Armed with these resources, they subjected a large part of the population of the earth to their colonial rule.

Yet, in gaining ascendancy, the West was actually advancing towards its own decline. During the centuries of Western dominance, Western technology, science, fashion and mentality spread throughout the world. This process of globalisation (or 'mondialisation') is accelerating. The world as a whole is undergoing rapid Westernisation.

This has led to the emergence of new powers outside of Europe. And this, in turn, has weakened the West's position in the world. We have now reached a point where the end of Western dominance is in sight.

Since the two World Wars the balance of power in the Western world has shifted from Europe to the United States. The United States has created a global empire, but competitors have arrived on the scene. China, India and Brazil have all emerged as superpowers. Russia is also a contender in the battle for global supremacy because of its mineral resources, and South Africa is clearly an economy to be reckoned with.

At a time when the balance of power is shifting throughout the world, we have witnessed the outbreak of a financial and economic crisis, which appears to be gradually escalating. I see this financial and economic crisis as an integral part of the general cultural crisis affecting the whole world. National leaders can no longer control the state of affairs in their country, nor can they control their country's banking system or its economy. And they are increasingly finding that they can no longer control the people they are supposed to rule. In our day it has become commonplace for a country to use violence against its own people.

An era is coming to an end. The crisis that heralds the end of an era is apparent throughout all aspects of culture. And as we witness the chaotic end of the 'modern era', we are also witnessing the collapse of the cornerstones of 'modern civilization': the 'modern' economy, 'modern' science and the 'modern' mentality.

Western ascendancy was made possible by modern culture. The question is, has the world outside the West something better to offer humanity? Have the people of non-Western nations developed plans that will help us create a more humane society?

If they have, I have yet to hear about it. The emerging nations use the same technology, the same science and the same economic model as the West. And they are rapidly adopting Western mentality. So a shift in the balance of power will essentially do little more than simply topple American supremacy.

We might also wonder what will be achieved by a battle for world power.

Superpowers rarely relinquish power voluntarily. And, far from considering the prospect, the Americans are actively amassing weapons. The way things currently stand, it seems humanity is about to face a global battle for power. Let us hope that such a battle does not degenerate into a war fought with weapons.

Unfortunately, it is probably more realistic to fear the

worst. World leaders are preparing to compete for global power with all the means at their disposal. Above all, they intend to use modern nuclear bombs, which are highly destructive. A Third World War will pretty much wipe out life on earth. It will mean the end of humanity.

38

When the outlook is bleak, saviours come to the rescue!

Dear Contemporaries,

Our global society is no longer capable of resolving the problems it faces. The existing financial and economic systems do not guarantee human happiness. The incidence of suicide is increasing. Corruption and crime have permeated all levels of society. In many countries people are taking to the streets to protest against injustice and oppression. There is widespread distrust. And there is no redeeming vision that promises a better future.

Since all countries are preoccupied with their own problems, issues that affect the world as a whole, such as pollution of the environment, the energy crisis, destruction of nature, the impending shortage of food and drinking water, the threat of epidemics, periodic famine and the need to mitigate climate change, remain unresolved. Every so often an international summit is convened to discuss one of these problems. Thousands of delegates and their support teams come together – and people are surprised when these spectacles fail to result in a fruitful outcome.

There is a stark and growing divide between rich and poor. This manifests within societies and across nations. Some nations possess great mineral wealth while others are deprived of these resources. Significant petroleum deposits in the Arab Gulf region have led Saudi Arabia and the other Gulf states to amass disproportionate wealth, while China, which has more than a billion inhabitants, has far fewer resources. This uneven distribution of resources will eventually become untenable.

It is not within the power of individual nations to heal

the global divide between rich and poor, or to solve other global problems. This can only be accomplished by a global authority. The fact that such an authority does not exist threatens to end in disaster.

In an era of global unification, the division of the surface of the earth into almost two hundred nations of varying sizes has become an anachronism. At this point in history, does the human race really need two hundred governments, two hundred bureaucracies, two hundred sets of armed forces, two hundred diplomatic corps and two hundred espionage networks?

Irrespective of the answer to this question, at the moment the human race is saddled with two hundred governments that do not agree. Given that this is the case, are we simply going to allow the problems of climate change, environmental pollution, destruction of nature, dwindling petroleum and other mineral resources, periodic famine, increasing poverty and wealth, international organised crime and economic depression to run their course? Are we simply going to accept the uneven distribution of political and military power? And are we going to refrain from doing anything to address the economic crisis that threatens the entire population of the earth with unemployment and impoverishment?

Of course not! When the outlook is bleak, eloquent individuals present themselves as leaders in a time of need. Autocratic leaders can always rise to power, but in times of crisis and despair they are far more likely to be well received. They appeal to latent primitive feelings and they can be recognised by their insistence on tyranny. They present themselves as saviours of their country and convince the people that the nation must be purged of foreign elements. The nation must be firmly united. They rouse the people to fight for victory in battle. Dissenters have to be eliminated because they undermine national unity and the power of the people. With leaders such as these in power, war is inevitable.

Their battle cry is loud and clear: Back to the animalism of the past!

But I would suggest a different motto. I say let's not wage war against our fellow human beings. Let's unite and work together to create a world that is more humane!

39

WORLD UNITY, NOW OR NEVER!

Dear Contemporaries,

Horde mentality is still alive and well in the world of national relations. Just as the members of a horde were often required to fight to the death if necessary, modern nations behave as if they are still in the jungle. States that wield power are gathering allies to fight alongside them in the forthcoming war. Armed conflict is spreading in certain regions. It is clearly only a matter of time before someone throws a spark into the gunpowder keg.

I know some people still cherish illusions about the power of the United Nations. They believe the United Nations is a kind of world government and that it will be able to prevent a Third World War. Or so they think.

Dear Contemporaries, Dear Readers, illusions won't get us very far. The United Nations is powerless as an organisation. This goes without saying, because this was the intention from the start. Who set up the United Nations with this intent? The prevailing superpowers. In today's world the prevailing superpowers call the shots, for the prevailing superpowers are the warlords of our day.

Only a powerful world government can put an end to the current anarchy. Global order can only be achieved by eliminating the sovereignty of existing nations and states. For the two hundred quarrelsome countries that span the globe are all sovereign entities. They can make their own rules, expand their own armed forces and pursue their own interests.

You might feel that this is what we all want, that national interests should come first. People of all countries are proud of their armed forces. They take pride in their national identity, their national culture, their national traditions and their monarchy or elected head of state. We sing our national anthems beneath our national flags. "We didn't ask for globalisation!" you might say. "Who says we have to agree to it? Surrender our sovereignty? Out of the question! We want to keep our own unique character. Our own people must come first!"

Yet, if you think about it, wouldn't it make more sense to do away with sovereign nations as soon as possible? Sovereign nations have clearly had their day. Wouldn't it be a blessing if war was banned once and for all?

But, for this to be possible, we must be very clear about how to proceed. All two hundred sovereign nations will have to disband their armed forces. There must be an end to the production and sale of weapons. All nuclear bombs and other weapons must be dismantled. All military academies must be closed. And, while we are closing obsolete institutions, we can also shut down all prisons for political opponents and all concentration camps.

Then our upbringing and education systems can take on a new focus: we can teach children the value of peace and respect for their fellow human beings throughout the world. We can raise them as humane citizens of the world. And at the same time we can also raise them to be people who make good use of all of their mental capacities, including their noetic capacity.

40

We are all members of the same family of man!

Dear Contemporaries,

You don't have to tell me that we cannot bring about world unity overnight. Long-established traditions endure. And these traditions include loyalty to one's own group, which automatically implies hostility towards those who are perceived as 'other'. Given that this is the case, quarrels between nations would appear to be permanently inevitable.

You will often hear it said that world unity would be a fine thing, but it is simply a utopian dream. I would counter this by saying that it is precisely because there is so much conflict that there needs to be an organisation that stands above warring factions – an organisation that possesses the power and the means to compel those who still wish to do battle to make peace. Of course this will only be possible if they have surrendered their weapons.

And are the world's hard-bitten statesmen queuing up impatiently to surrender their weapons? Far from it! The motto of every statesman is "We will never surrender! We are in the right! We have the right to defend our own interests with tooth and nail. Long live the Fatherland! Long live the nation! We will show no mercy to nations that stand in our way!

Yes, I am well aware that we face a gargantuan task if we want to create a peaceful world. But that is not a good reason for us to sit down and do nothing. The global population must realise that, as well as nationalists, there are also mondialists. There are people who want world unity.

In other words, mondialists in all countries will need

to make themselves known. It will be a historic moment when they unite behind a global mondialist organisation, a World Unity Movement.

Firstly the members of a World Unity Movement will make it clear to their contemporaries that humanity has to choose between world unity and world destruction, because world unity is the necessary prerequisite for world peace.

Secondly they will help the world population understand how we can create the global unity that the Family of Man needs by setting up an organisation that has the power and the means to find sustainable solutions to the series of global problems we now face.

And thirdly a World Unity Movement will offer every human being the prospect of a safe and dignified existence. The movement will break new ground in this respect for it will be the first political movement in history to promote the interests of humanity as a whole.

This hypothetical future will become a reality once all people understand that we, the inhabitants of the earth, are all members of the same family, the Family of Man.

41

You too can help to create unity and peace!

Dear Reader,

Time is running out. The cultural crisis is threatening to get worse. A new world will emerge from the ashes of the chaos we see around us. But this will not happen by itself.

Society and culture are created by human beings. If we feel that our current society has become untenable, we ourselves will have to build a better society.

And we can. We possess the faculties we need to do this. We can distance ourselves from everything that divides humanity – even if all kinds of people seek to convince us that we have to fight each other to the death.

The cultural crisis of our time is entering the stage of 'prevolution', a stage characterised by increasing unrest and resistance. Attempts to introduce positive changes that focus on problems of the moment in a certain region or country will never lead to a lasting solution. They will simply add to the sense of disorder and despair.

A turning point will have been reached once we embark on a process of deep reflection on the global task now facing humanity. This process of reflection will require that we identify the dictates we want to live by in shaping our culture. We will need to access deeper insight than can be afforded by our current thinking. The desire to ensure the continued existence of our culture at a better and higher level will inevitably lead to a form of metabletic thinking.

We will begin to see the end of the cultural crisis once a global movement guided by metabletic and mondialist principles has spread to all countries. And we will have emerged from the cultural crisis once we have appointed a global authority with the power to guide cultural evolution on earth.

A World Unity Movement will play a decisive role in this process and it will need to draw up plans to achieve its aims. These plans will address the appointment of a world government and the fundamental renewal of society. They will be the most comprehensive plans ever formulated. For the first time in history there will be a global discussion about the world of tomorrow.

Our upbringing and education systems will also need to play a decisive role in this process - and they must. They must serve as the catalyst that makes the current global population less primitive. And they can fulfil this task by introducing less primitive thinking, breaking with obsolete traditions, making new generations aware of humankind's tremendous potencies, eliminating the horde mentality that seeks to serve the interests of a separate group and doing everything to make people understand that we, the inhabitants of the earth, all belong to one family, the Family of Man.

My dear Contemporaries, in writing these letters I have endeavoured to set my personal interests aside in order to serve the interests of my family. And, as far as I am concerned, my family is and will always be the Family of Man.

May we see the formation of a World Unity Movement without delay!

Dear Reader, I hope I have offered you a vision that you feel is worth aspiring to and working towards!

Epilogue

Dear Reader,

I have written you quite a lot of letters. Did I really have to write so many? Yes, I think so. For most of my life – and it has been a long one – I have been trying to create a vision of hope for the future. It has taken me a long time to achieve what I set out to do because I wish to offer a vision that is both realistic and attainable. In fact, it is only now, at my advanced age, as I look back on my quest, that I see just how many problems and hindrances there were. These included the following:

It seemed to me that, in order to gain a clearer understanding of our own era, it is essential that we distance ourselves as much as possible – at least in our thinking – from what is happening in the human world and that we reflect on the vast world that surrounds us. I think it's unfortunate that we do this so rarely, because it expands our view. And it does this in two different ways.

Firstly, we begin to get a sense of the vast expanse of cosmic space and we realise that what happens on earth is relatively unimportant on a cosmic scale.

Secondly, it expands our concept of time. Billions of years have elapsed since the big bang occurred. If we stop to consider this, we realise that there are developments that take place over very long periods. I am talking about evolutionary changes. This is by no means a new idea, but it is certainly worth reflecting on. It was this idea that led me to renew my thinking.

Science acknowledges that evolution is a universal phenomenon but it stops there. In other words, the ramifications of this realisation have not been adequately thought through. This is a mistake we make at our own peril. Because in failing to fully appreciate the universal nature of evolution, we remain unaware of the extent to which we are limited by our current way of thinking. We are immersed in and part of a dynamic reality, yet our thinking is static. We keep trying to ascertain reality. We tell ourselves, "This is the way it is!" Yet rather than thinking in moving images, we think in individual frames as it were. I believe this kind of static thinking needs to be abandoned and replaced by dynamic metabletic thinking – a way of thinking that recognises and allows for the fact that reality is constantly changing and evolving.

It is static thinking that leads scientists to maintain that no matter how much evolution occurs it can never lead to the emergence of essential change. They continue to assert the principle of the uniformity of nature. Evolutionary changes may be quantitative, but they never introduce a qualitative or essential difference.

In my view nothing could be further from the truth. Those who are willing to look reality in the face see that the cosmos, the universe as a whole, evolves in stages, and that each new stage is characterised by new possibilities or capacities: new potencies in other words. The principle of uniformity is a fallacy. Increasing potentiation is a fundamental law of reality. A basic understanding of this fundamental law should be adopted as the starting point of any and all scientific philosophy.

The worldview that emerges from this kind of dynamic metabletic thinking is that of a cosmos made up of series of spheres of progressing potency. These spheres include, among others, a subatomic sphere, an atomic sphere, a chemosphere and a biosphere. Each new sphere is characterised by the fact that it possesses a wider range of potencies and more advanced potencies than the sphere out of which it emerges.

Given that this is the case, we need to revise our view of humankind to make it consistent with this worldview. From a metabletic perspective, the fact that human beings appeared on the evolutionary scene relatively recently implies that they possess exceptional potencies. This is indeed the case. These exceptional potencies are humankind's mental capacities. The surprising conclusion is that evolution after creating a biosphere proceeded with the formation of a psychosphere.

There have clearly been evolutionary changes within the psychosphere itself. The first mental capacity to emerge was probably empathy: a potency that enables sentient beings to communicate with their surroundings by unconsciously merging with their environment. Another mental potency, which emerged together with the distance senses of sight and hearing, encompasses a series of conscious capacities that can be grouped under the heading of epistemic ability. This series of hypotheses then leads to the assertion that higher mammals and human beings possess a third mental potency: they are endowed with a noetic faculty, created by the synthesis of the two preceding potencies. In common parlance we refer to human noetic capacity as the mind. And the human mind a set of faculties of a higher order than the component potencies that combine to create it. It is actually the most powerful potency we know of.

As human beings we are part of nature, yet we occupy a unique position in this respect. Our bodies and our brains exist within the biosphere, yet our mind exists within a higher sphere: the psychosphere. This understanding finally provides an answer to the age-old question about the relationship between the mind and the brain.

The static thinking that seeks to ascertain reality leads to a static worldview. And that is not all. It also leads us to confuse our image of reality with reality itself. Those who say, "This is the way it is!" make no distinction between their thoughts about reality and reality itself. We reify our ideas. In other words, we treat abstract concepts as if they are real. We do this in our daily lives and it is also something that happens in science.

The process of reification occasionally leads to absurd notions. This happens when we reify concepts such as time and space. These concepts do not belong to the realm of nature; they are part of the world of physics. But what does Einstein do? He reifies his mathematical description of the cosmos, including the abstract notions of time and space. He tells us that time can speed up and slow down and that space is curved. Yet a metableticist will tell us that nature does not consist of mathematical formulas: it consists of reality. So my advice to scientists would be to draw a line under the thinking that seeks to ascertain reality and leads to reification once and for all, and to engage in metabletic thinking. If people follow this advice, thousands of years of mistaking models of reality for reality itself will finally come to an end.

The ideational and material creations of the human mind can all be grouped under the heading of culture. With the advent of culture, rather than being created by nature, new potencies are now created by humankind. The sphere of culture has triumphed to such an extent that it is now systematically depleting the older spheres of potency on earth. Plant and animal species are being wiped out and mineral resources are being consumed at an unsustainable rate. Yet universal evolution bestows upon humankind the historic task of stewarding the ongoing evolution of human culture and the natural world. Is the current global population adequately prepared and equipped to carry out this task? Not as things stand.

Of course the task itself is not an easy one. The performance of such a task requires profound insight and understanding. And only once such insight and understanding have been gained will humankind be fully aware of the extent of the global problems. Only then will people understand that these problems can only be overcome by a united humanity. Human culture as it currently exists meets neither of these conditions. Our scientific thinking is still too primitive and the willingness to work towards global political unity is entirely lacking. No plans are being drawn up to safeguard the future of humanity.

This means that as a global community we are faced with three tasks. Firstly, we need to move beyond the primitiveness of the current scientific paradigm. Secondly, we need to develop a mindset consistent with true humanity and global solidarity. And thirdly, we need to establish a political order that will safeguard the preservation of unity and world peace. These three processes of global reform will need to be implemented in conjunction with each other so they reinforce each other.

In short, three things are now required: 1. Deeper insight and understanding, 2. The humanisation of society, and 3. Global political unity.

1. Deeper insight and understanding

We lack understanding of the nature of reality. This is especially true of the phenomenon of culture. I am convinced that a metabletic approach will enable us to deepen our understanding of human evolution and human society. We need to create a new discipline, a science of culture, in which we study culture as a sphere of potency.

An initial articulation of a science of culture will immediately make it clear that human cultural evolution consists of three distinct stages. The first is the Animalium, an era of animal existence. Those days have gone. Humans transcended animal existence and created culture. Since then we have been evolving towards the Humanium, at which point humans will have shed their animal traits. At the moment we are still in a transitional stage, the Transitium.

During this Transitium true civilization has yet to be established. The term implies the existence of a highly developed culture. But human culture as it currently exists is still in its infancy. It is easy to understand why this is the case, given that it is only a few hundred generations since the sphere of culture emerged from the earliest forms of agriculture and livestock farming. In terms of evolutionary time frames this is a very short period. The relative immaturity of human culture means that people often still display animal behaviour and that our culture is still primitive.

There is one remarkable exception that stands out against this primitiveness, and that is the surprising advancement of technology. In creating culture humans have achieved their greatest successes at a material level. Over the course of a few hundred centuries this technological potentiation has created the phenomenon of affluence. And in creating affluence we have left animal existence far behind us. Affluence is now spreading throughout the globe at an ever-increasing rate.

Ironically this period of accelerating cultural evolution is also marked by a countermovement characterised by the resurgence of primitive ideas and behaviours. Yet from a metabletic point of view this can be explained by the fact that, like all other forms of evolution, cultural evolution occasionally goes through periods of crisis in which newly emerging values clash with long-standing traditions. This is what is now happening. What we are seeing is certainly not only a financial and economic crisis. Chaotic situations, war, mass murder, acts of violence, moral corruption and crime, all of which are occurring on a massive scale, are symptomatic of a general cultural crisis. And a crisis of this magnitude cannot be overcome with a few ad hoc measures. What is required is a complete and profound revolution in our way of thinking.

From the perspective of cultural science this raises a question. Assuming that humankind is able to overcome this global crisis, will it then be able to cross the threshold to the Humanium? It seems possible. The objective conditions are present. A revolution in our way of thinking, such as the one I have described, could be the gateway to a higher stage of culture, the gateway to a new era. An era of greater understanding, peace and human solidarity. An era in which human beings start to shape the course of evolution on earth.

2. The humanisation of society

We live in a world dominated by primitive impulses, such as the desire to engage in conflict, barbarity, ruthlessness, hostility towards those perceived as 'other', intolerance, abuse of power and status, competitiveness that will stop at nothing, aggression, violence, and the need to humiliate, torment and destroy those perceived as 'other'. These primitive animal traits of our culture dominate our news headlines.

This is actually not that surprising. There is always a tendency to regress to more primitive levels of functioning in times of crisis. The cultural crisis of our time will go down in history as a period of tyranny, unscrupulous pursuit of wealth, concentration camps, mass destruction of human life, war atrocities, violent oppression, organised crime and the development of increasingly elaborate and effective instruments of war.

Times of crisis also tend to be characterised by unbridled competition. In the corporate sphere employees fight for the best-paid jobs, sport is often an arena where aggressive rivalries are played out, artists enter countless competitions to compete for first prize, and the members of political parties engage in intrigue and machinations to their hearts' content. Nations threaten and go to war with each other to acquire or secure possession of mineral resources or strategic locations, or to establish hegemony in a part of the world or even world dominance.

The problem of 'us' and 'them' is a particularly acute issue. Mondialisation involves migration, which means that people are directly confronted with traditions and customs that differ from their own. These differences are often met with aversion and resistance. This is why we are now seeing a resurgence of horde mentality, which manifests in attitudes and behaviours that express hate and hostility towards those perceived as 'other', usually people of a different colour or faith, people with different customs who speak a different language and have a different mentality.

The conclusion is irrefutable. As in every crisis, renewal is encountering opposition - often violent opposition. And this is unlikely to change while people continue to rely on static freeze-frame thinking.

With all of this going on, it is clear that the humanisation process that began with the advent of culture has virtually come to a standstill and occasionally appears to be completely absent. The atrocities committed in the era in which we live are far worse than anything that happened in the past. This is because the mechanisation and computerisation facilitated by modern technology now enable us to kill each other in unprecedented numbers. Statesmen rarely feel hampered by humanitarian considerations, especially in times of crisis. Nations sometimes behave like crime syndicates. We are surrounded by injustice and lawlessness on all sides.

As far as I know, there is no national constitution that lists the building of a humane society as one of its aspirations. Constitutions do not mention the word humanity. At best they define human rights. The language and conceptual frameworks used by governments reduce the idea of true humanity to a legal concept. Barbarity simply exists as a 'violation of human rights'. But true humanity is not something that can be imposed by law. It lives in people's hearts. Unfortunately man's animal nature is often more apparent than his human nature. We live in an inhumane world.

3. Global political unity

As far as the future political order is concerned, humanity is faced with the task of resolving global problems. And the problems are considerable. Mondialisation brings together people of very different cultures. This sparks a widespread sense of unease and negative reactions that stem from an ancient code of group loyalty. Those who are perceived as 'other' are always thought to be the ones causing the problem. They are a threat to the unique cultural character of the group. The understanding that at this point in history we are called upon to forge cultural unity has yet to materialise. People have yet to realise that there is a moral imperative for humankind to make a global effort to shape the ongoing evolution of the sphere of culture and raise it to a higher level.

Political leaders who use the widespread feelings of unease for own purposes are partly to blame for the absence of any serious endeavour to create unity. Political leaders deliberately play on people's attachment to traditions and their need to be part of a group, in this case the nation. Leaders who appeal to these conservative impulses always draw a wide response. Any advance towards global political unity is inconceivable as things stand because the opponents of this movement - those who advocate traditionalism and nationalism - are the overriding factor in the political dynamics of each country because of their massive numbers.

Traditionalism, the desire to preserve established ideas

and customs, sometimes assumes extreme forms in our time. In the Islamic world, but not only there, we have seen a return to orthodox customs of the distant past. And traditionalism is often the ideological engine that drives political activity, which sometimes degenerates into violence and terrorism.

Nationalism is a more recent phenomenon. At the top of the nationalist agenda is the desire to establish an independent sovereign state for the nation. Since decolonisation, the whole world has been divided into sovereign nations. The citizens of each state expect their leaders to defend the interests of their own nation – national interests.

National interests are, by definition, group interests. As such, they are diametrically opposed to the direction in which cultural evolution is moving. In other words, at a time when global unity is required, nationalism is a notion that impedes progress. Worse still, it is also a danger to humanity. As the defenders of national interests, statesmen can use nationalist slogans to generate widespread popular support for aggressive plans. These slogans always say more or less the same thing: 'Our own people come first!'

Nations still harbour the horde mentality that dates back to the days of the Animalium. Back then the members of the horde knew that their only hope of survival in the jungle depended on their ability to form a tight-knit group. They revered the leader of the horde and offered him their unconditional obedience. If necessary, they sacrificed their own lives for the horde. Today's nation states are the tight-knit group that has to defend itself in the vicious jungle of power politics. People gather around a national leader and a national flag. They celebrate national holidays, sing national anthems and pay tribute to national heroes in patriotic verses and songs. And, if necessary, they sacrifice their lives to defend the interests of their people and their fatherland.

All existing political practice is, without exception, the practice of power politics. People seek to make their nation strong, firstly by promoting economic development. They regard their national armed forces as a powerful asset, they prepare for war and form military alliances. This so-called defence policy is largely based on the work of espionage services and diplomacy. As a result, the world of international politics is still a jungle, in which nations are perpetually involved in a power struggle.

The practice of power politics is inevitable in a world divided into a multitude of sovereign nations. Sovereign states will always feel compelled to defend their national interests. Yet in an era when rapid development of nuclear bombs and long range missiles is the order of the day, the existence of a multitude of sovereign nations could lead to a global catastrophe. A global nuclear war could destroy all culture. And possibly even wipe out the human race.

If we want to put an end to the practice of power politics, it is imperative that we put an end to the sovereignty of individual nation states. National sovereignty will need to be transferred to a global authority, a world government. Only a world government will be able to maintain global order, guarantee peace and resolve global problems.

Dear Readers,

I am calling for us to put an end to nationalism and to embrace mondialism. Rather than defending the interests of a particular nation, it is time for us to start safeguarding and furthering the interests of humankind as a whole.

If this is an idea that appeals to you, I invite you to help set up a World Unity Movement. The ultimate aims of such a movement are still a long way from being achieved. Where should the movement start? I think it would have to start by fostering a sense of global unity. How? Allow me to make a few suggestions off the top of my head.

The Olympic Games, in their current form, are an opportunity for every nation to show the world what it is capable of in terms of athletic excellence. Champions are revered because, through the eye of the television camera, they are perceived as heroes by a global television audience. They are decorated with medals and become national demigods during the hoisting of the national flag and the playing of the national anthem. In other words, the Olympic Games, in their current form, continue to promote competition between nations. They are all about a display of national ability, and demonstrating to the world that the nation is as good as, if not better than, other nations. In short, the Olympic Games are essentially an orgy of nationalism. But they don't have to be. The Olympic Games could be transformed into a celebration of global solidarity. Surely this is a possibility that deserves some thought!

It would also help to create a sense of unity if those who feel an affinity with the ideals of mondialism were to campaign for equal rights for men, women and children throughout the world. This is one of the principles enshrined in the

Universal Declaration of Human Rights adopted by the United Nations General Assembly back in 1948. The fact that so little has been done to make this principle a reality in the intervening years simply testifies to the powerlessness of the United Nations as an international organisation.

Another point worth mentioning is that the global corporate sector would benefit from the standardisation of weights and measures. And it will also become clear that global standardisation in other areas is not simply a luxury.

And a final tip. The mondialists have devised a World Calendar. The calendar is neutral in every respect, which should make it acceptable to everyone on the planet. It is also more efficient than our existing calendars. If this World Calendar is introduced, the whole of humankind will celebrate the same global holiday at least once a year. The appendix that follows explains the advantages of a World Calendar.

If you would like to come into contact with others who feel an affinity with the ideals of mondialism, please visit the Mankind United website, www.mankindunited.org

World Calendar

Four identical quarters

JANUARY

S	M	T	W	T	F	S
1	2	3	4	5	6	7
8	9	10	11	12	13	14
15	16	17	18	19	20	21
22	23	24	25	26	27	28
29	30	31				

FEBRUARY

S	M	T	W	T	F	S
			1	2	3	4
5	6	7	8	9	10	11
12	13	14	15	16	17	18
19	20	21	22	23	24	25
26	27	28	29	30		

MARCH

S	M	T	W	T	F	S
					1	2
3	4	5	6	7	8	9
10	11	12	13	14	15	16
17	18	19	20	21	22	23
24	25	26	27	28	29	30

APRIL

S	M	T	W	T	F	S
1	2	3	4	5	6	7
8	9	10	11	12	13	14
15	16	17	18	19	20	21
22	23	24	25	26	27	28
29	30	31				

MAY

S	M	T	W	T	F	S
			1	2	3	4
5	6	7	8	9	10	11
12	13	14	15	16	17	18
19	20	21	22	23	24	25
26	27	28	29	30		

JUNE

S	M	T	W	T	F	S
					1	2
3	4	5	6	7	8	9
10	11	12	13	14	15	16
17	18	19	20	21	22	23
24	25	26	27	28	29	30

JULY

S	M	T	W	T	F	S
1	2	3	4	5	6	7
8	9	10	11	12	13	14
15	16	17	18	19	20	21
22	23	24	25	26	27	28
29	30	31				

AUGUST

S	M	T	W	T	F	S
			1	2	3	4
5	6	7	8	9	10	11
12	13	14	15	16	17	18
19	20	21	22	23	24	25
26	27	28	29	30		

SEPTEMBER

S	M	T	W	T	F	S
					1	2
3	4	5	6	7	8	9
10	11	12	13	14	15	16
17	18	19	20	21	22	23
24	25	26	27	28	29	30

OCTOBER

S	M	T	W	T	F	S
1	2	3	4	5	6	7
8	9	10	11	12	13	14
15	16	17	18	19	20	21
22	23	24	25	26	27	28
29	30	31				

NOVEMBER

S	M	T	W	T	F	S
			1	2	3	4
5	6	7	8	9	10	11
12	13	14	15	16	17	18
19	20	21	22	23	24	25
26	27	28	29	30		

DECEMBER

S	M	T	W	T	F	S
					1	2
3	4	5	6	7	8	9
10	11	12	13	14	15	16
17	18	19	20	21	22	23
24	25	26	27	28	29	30

How the calendar works

The calendar is based on the following principles:
1. The calendar is ideologically neutral.
2. The calendar is more efficient than our existing calendars.

Ideological neutrality
The only public holiday is a Mid-Year Day. Of course, every culture is free to designate its own preferred public holidays. The global community will have to decide when the World Calendar is to be introduced.

Efficiency
The World Calendar follows the solar year. Efficiency is achieved as follows:

- There are four quarters that each consist of 91 days. in each quarter there are two 30-day months and one 31-day month. There are 13 weeks in each quarter. And each quarter begins with he first day of the week and ends with the last day of the week.

- Four quarters that each consist of 91 days fill 364 days of the year. The solar year is completed by adding two additional days, which fall outside the recurring pattern of weeks, months and quarters.

- The first additional day is a day that is scheduled every year. Mondialists propose that this day should be scheduled between the second and third quarters and celebrated as World Unity Day.

- The second additional day is a leap year day, which can be scheduled in the same way that leap years are scheduled in the Gregorian calendar. In other words, a leap year day is scheduled if the last two figures of the year are divisible by four, unless the last two figures of the year are 00, in which case an exception applies if the first two figures of the year are divisible by four.

- If, in the future, the world community decides to reduce the number of days in a week from seven to six, there will then be precisely five weeks in each month and 90 days in each quarter. The 91st day could then be scheduled as an additional day. If the number of days in a week is reduced to five, there will then be six weeks in a month and 90 days in a quarter. Again the 91st day could be scheduled as an additional day.

The efficiency of the World Calendar is clear: there is a consistent relationship between the day of the year, the day of the week and the day of the month. Each year repeats exactly the same pattern.